NEESHA M. STRINGFELLOW

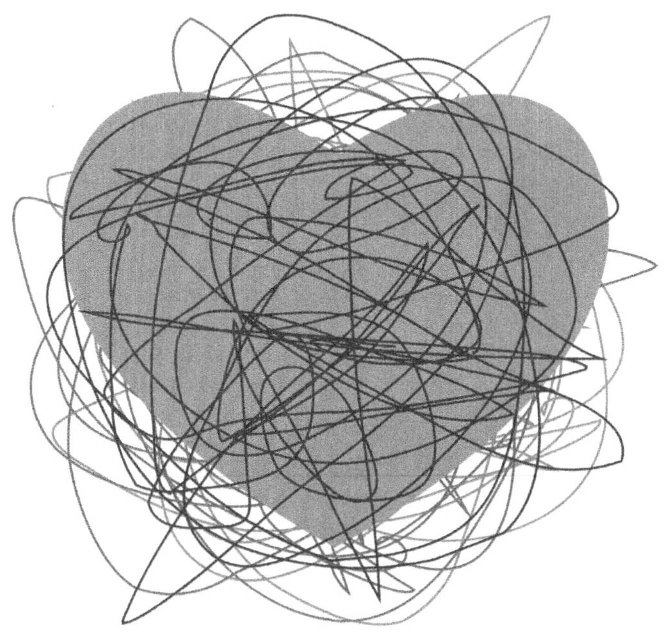

RELATIONSHIPS DRIVING ME CRAZY!

God's Love Heals

Relationships Driving Me Crazy!
God's Love Heals

NEESHA M. STRINGFELLOW
neeshasnetwork@gmail.com

ISBN 978-1-943343-60-7
Printed in the USA.

Published by: Destined To Publish | Flossmoor, Illinois
www.DestinedToPublish.com

Dedication

I honor and appreciate my relationship with my Lord and Savior, Jesus Christ. This is the most important relationship in my life overall. I honor the Heavenly Father for being mindful of man and creating relationships.

I dedicate this book to my best friend. The one who has been consistent in my life for over thirty-five years. My husband, Wesley Stringfellow, thank you for loving me, choosing me first, and caring about my needs. It never goes unnoticed how you give unselfishly to me along with our family and friends.

From our humble beginnings of marriage, you have loved me like Christ loves the church. Thank you for walking in integrity and showing me what real love is in the human form. I celebrate you and honor you.

May your days be filled with love, laughter, excellent health, and prosperity. May God continue to give you grace in every area of your life. You are my guy til death do us part! I love you, Wesley Stringfellow.

Love your best friend

~ Neesha

PROLOGUE

God's Love Letter

Dear Beloved,

I love you my child, I want you to know me; I want you and have wanted you from the beginning, to have the kind of relationship that spins you out of control, the one that makes your heartbeat fast when I am talking to you, or when you hear people mention my name you know that you belong to me. I knew you before I formed you in your mother's womb. You were my idea. I want you to know that no matter how many struggles you have in life I will always be here for you to carry you through.

When I created man, my plan was for you to live a life filled with joy and no sorrow. Sin entered the world and changed my original plan for mankind. The love I have for you has never changed and is never ending. I know life is bound to throw some painful experiences your way, but always remember you can come to me, I am here to comfort, repair, mend and heal your heart. Sometimes you don't have words to express how you feel about me, sometimes you can even be angry with me due to circumstances you don't understand. You might even blame me and never want to speak with me again.

My child, never fear, my thoughts are high above your thoughts and my ways are far above your ways. Therefore, you must understand that the hidden treasures of my love for you are found in my word. The way I feel about you is described in my love letter to you. Come into my presence and you will find the peace and the love you need to fill your days with joy. Draw close to me, your relationship with me is so important. It is imperative to make time with me every day, and at all times of the day. Make sure you pause to talk to me and connect with me. I love you so much.

Love, Daddy God

Contents

Foreword vii

Introduction xv

Relationships Are Driving Me Crazy 1

Relationships: Whose Idea Was It Anyway? 9

Still Driving Me Crazy! 17

Waiting on You 27

Crazy Determination 33

Relationship Baggage 41

Marriage and Other Relationship Ideas 49

Rescue Me! 55

Reboot Your Relationships 69

Grace Grace Grace 77

The Great Escape 85

Emotions 99

Crisis Relationships / Cry-Sees
(Answering the Cry) 115

Breaking The Cycle of Crazy 125

Restored Relationships 133

Crazy to Healed 151

Acknowledgments 155

FOREWORD

By my Hubby and Best Friend, Wesley Stringfellow

On any given day you can probably walk into just about any major bookstore and throw a handful of darts and hit at least one book on relationships. This is not necessarily a bad thing. I believe even in this time with social media, remote working, remote meetings, remote learning, remote worship, and all the remote movies and media available at the click of a button, it would almost seem to appear that we rarely get to enjoy the companionship of other people face to face.

My wife Neesha, who is a wife, mother, author, successful business owner, and business and relationship coach, has written this book from her own personal relationships with friends and family. If anyone knows Neesha, then they know how important every single one of her relationships is and how much she values them. Throughout these chapters Neesha will show you how to successfully navigate through all types of relationships, whether they are family, romantic relationships, friend, or business.

All relationships are important in your journey through life. You will also learn that not all relationships are pillars in your life and were not meant to be permanent. Some were just supporting posts only, set in place to hold you up temporarily. You will discover that some relationships were toxic, and it was you that held on far too long. Most importantly, you will discover how to manage your current relationships by understanding what your response should be and why.

Neesha Stringfellow is truly a relationship expert. She looks beyond what we typically see on the surface and dives into a deeper understanding of the root of people's experiences that shaped them to be who they are. There is a popular saying, "Knowing is half the battle," and when you can see past the surface and understand the other person, and most importantly understand yourself at a deeper level, it will allow "Grace" to take place.

So please do yourself a favor and study this book with a group or by yourself. It will be life changing, and the life you change will be your own!

Reflections by Neesha

I share these intimate moments with you about my crazy relationship with myself and with sitting down long enough to see that sometimes I was a basket of emotions, sometimes I was excited, sometimes I blamed others, and all the time I just wanted to be done with this book. The reflections below are from some of my emotions while writing in my journals throughout the years of trying to complete this book. It's always a great idea to go back and reflect on the progress you have made, especially when you have finally come to completion. I am grateful for my journey, although I am still hard on myself thinking that I should have been done with this project a long time ago. Yet, God has had me this entire time, and I pray that "my CRAZY journey" will bless you. These are excerpts from my journals, and as you read them, I urge you to begin or continue journaling. For every journal is a publication from you.

2022

This part right here is super funny. I have reflected on the idea of finishing this book and starting and stopping 1000 times. My journals are all half full since I am a person who must have something fresh when I sit down to write. A fresh new journal calls out to me while standing in the aisle at a Marshalls or TJ Maxx and says, "*pick me up*". I decide to indulge and fill my cart up with not just one but a minimum of two new journals so I can start journaling again. I pray in these journals, I take notes, write my "things to do" lists, and I just can't wait to sit down and start again. I always get a good start and then life gets in the way and my journaling every day turns to maybe every week which slips into every other month, and then I look around and the brand-new journal I was super excited about has sat next to my favorite chair, or my quiet place where I spend time with God, for about a year. I often ask myself if this will ever change. I am grateful that I finally took some time to sit down today and journaled the completion of to the first part of this manuscript.

Who is my audience? Everyone who has encountered a "crazy" in their relationships. I pray people will be blessed by my transparency. Daddy God will you please bless this project? Will you please allow me to grow and to know that it is because of you that I am able to write out my thoughts and then rejoice in knowing that I have the privilege to share them through publishing all that's been on my heart ... until next journal?

2021

Lord, what are you saying? My own personal relationship with you seems to be okay. I mean I think I heard you clearly, but I must admit just knowing that is not good enough. I need a deeper relationship with you. I need to hear you and believe when you have spoken to me that it's real. I must not waiver in my belief. I will begin to encourage myself, I know I cannot do things within my own strength. It is my spiritual and natural DNA that you gave me that constantly causes me to rethink, reboot, and finally know that God will work things out.

So, sitting in front of the computer once again and repeating over and over in my head, "If I ever complete this book, I will be so appreciative," and talking to myself of how I need to have another month or year of quiet for successful completion, I realize it's me who chooses the busy, it's me who needs to say "no" to the many demands in life.

No one else can do that for me.

If you haven't started journaling yet, start today.

2019

It's another one of those days when my relationship with myself is having a battle. Trying to find time for me, myself, and I, and learning that if I don't put myself first, I will be upset with who, today? In life we put the blame game on everyone and everything when we see that we have left things incomplete or are left unfulfilled. However, who is really the culprit? I'm quite sure I can say, "Me, myself, and I!" I find fault in my relationship with me daily, and I need to get off that hamster wheel. The relationship with myself is sometimes very good. I think personally I find myself rather productive, and I always challenge myself to have integrity and make sure I do my best to keep my word. However, "I" can be lazy at times, find excuses to waste valuable working time, saying again, why don't "I" complete what "I" started. Why don't "I" dedicate the time "I" need for Neesha? Well, the deadline is rapidly approaching, I'm running out of excuses and Me, Myself, and I must promise to complete this work.

September 20, 2019

My fiftieth birthday is my deadline to have this on paper and published. I have so many things on my plate. I have announced it, so I must have it finished. Why? Because my word is my bond! *Right?* I mean when you promise not only yourself but others, you must be accountable to completing what you said you would do. Why the rush? I'm not sure. I just want to set this goal in place and accomplish it by a set time. God give me the strength to not have a scatterbrain and to relax in your presence, knowing you have it all under control.

December 1, 2019

Well, another birthday has come and gone, and my goal was not completed. My task did not get accomplished. I am, however, grateful for life. My golden birthday is here, and I am grateful that I have made it to see this beautiful day. Writing this book has made me realize I have more challenged relationships than I care to admit; however, I realize it was my own letdown that has hurt me more. I have decided to give it to God and go back and reflect on one of my favorite passages:

"He has made everything beautiful in its time." (Ecclesiastes 3:11 KJV)

Journaling doesn't have to be long, but it must be written. A few words can bring back moments that remind us why we are purposed to be here and how we best contribute to the relationships around us in our day-to-day lives. It is also a chronological account of how life doesn't happen according to my timetable and neither do my relationships happen the way that I want them to happen. Journaling reminds me that the best parts of any relationship happen on God's time.

So again, I admit, it's not my timing but it's God's timing. I am learning to lean on and trust Him in everything and every relationship.

_2017_

Whether it means rising early or going to bed a little later, the moments I need to complete anything, belong to me. Praying for the grace of time is all good, but if I never take the time to-do what I set out to do then no one is to blame but me. I stole this time away, and it took so much time to wind down that now my deadline is almost here, and I have become a little anxious in hoping this is the longest day ever. My pen seems to be automatic, and my words are flowing onto the pages with ease. I'm praying to God that He will miraculously extend the hours in this day.

2016

Well, I have come to realize that it's taking me too long to complete this book. The main reason is because of the many distractions that I put in the way of completing it. Yes, I said it, I put the distractions in the way, and the biggest distraction has been me. Procrastinating and trying to figure out if this is really something I need to do. Sometimes the distractions can be life-altering, unexpected experiences. This year was probably one of the hardest I have ever had to encounter. Sickness, death, and life all at the same time. I struggled with our creator, my heavenly Father, this year. I was disappointed by the way things turned out. I trust you, Father, but I don't like it.

This book has been long coming, and I only hope it can be a tool to give people a different perspective in understanding the dynamics of relationships. Honestly, there will never be a perfect relationship; there may be moments of joy and happiness and bliss, but in every relationship, there will be trials and some form of feathers ruffled, to put it lightly.

2015

A new year has arrived, and I have become even more antsy and frustrated, thinking it's about others not wanting to jump on board with the vision God has given me to write this book on relationships. It appeared that even my husband and co-laborers were not excited about the call of God on my life. Recognizing I have had a great support system, I must revaluate things. My speech must change, my thoughts must become one and line up with God's word.

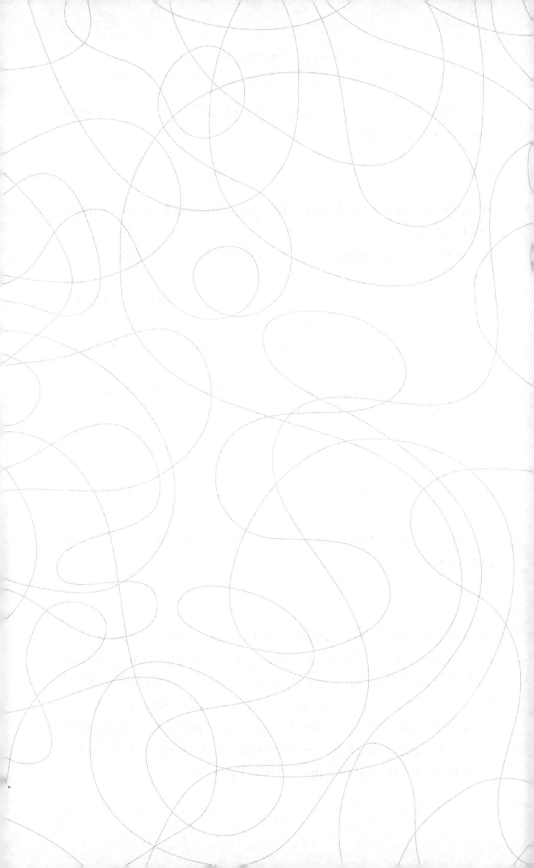

Introduction

Crazy!

Now don't be alarmed by the word crazy; it's a mere figure of speech. People use the term loosely, and most of the time it is not used in a literal way. In Merriam Webster's dictionary, the term crazy is defined several ways. First, it is defined as being full of cracks or flaws, something unsound. That is not the definition I connected with when I used it in the title of this book. Another definition says that crazy can mean crooked or askew, while another description says crazy means impractical or erratic. None of these fit my definition.

I'm sharing all of these so you will truly grasp the difference in the way I use the term crazy. The above definitions for crazy don't lean into my meaning, so hopefully I will draw you closer to the meaning as we look at another dictionary which says crazy can mean unusual, infatuated, obsessed to an extreme degree, and wildly extreme. I want to make sure you know, when I use the term 'crazy' that it means all these things to me. In relationships, we are Crazy to think, Crazy to love, Crazy to learn, Crazy to cry, Crazy to pray, Crazy to laugh, Crazy to live! It is an intense thing, obsessive at times, and wildly extreme.

The Crazy experiences life offers don't necessarily make us lose our minds and they don't literally drive us insane, but they do cause us to consider the extremes they take us into, and how that impacts our lives. But it is the moment in our lives we need to take a moment to pause.

What is it about relationships that drive me crazy? We all have moments that can take us to a point where we need to pause and breathe. Examining our 'crazy' can allow you to reflect and especially pray.

By delving into our relationships with people, places, and things, and learning how to cope with them, can lead us into a time of re-thinking or re-evaluating the experiences associated with them. A real excitement comes when we recognized we have gained a lesson from each one of those relationships, and recognizing that those experiences that come with every relationship have purpose.

As I have matured in my faith in God, I have been taught many things. I'm still learning, but one thing that has helped me to continue to grow in my relationships has been having a personal relationship with Jesus Christ. Accepting Him as my Lord and Savior is the one relationship, I know that I want and need. Knowing that He loves me and wants the best for me is probably the best part of the relationship.

I also thank God that He is not wishy washy like me and Jesus's love for me is unconditional. In my own prayer time and relationship with Jesus, I often apologize when I think on my shortcomings. I know that I drive Him crazy at times, but I also follow up with the comment that "Daddy, I know you know me, for you created me ."

In this book, I pray you define "crazy" in your relationships. And with that you will always remember that you can navigate through them all when you have the most important relationship of all, being one with Jesus. Discover and continue to rediscover your walk with Jesus.

Chapter One

Relationships Are Driving Me Crazy

As human beings we need certain tangible things, ideas, and inventions to bring our thoughts to life. Some of the smartest people in the world are those who are gifted in the wonderful world of technology and electronic devices. People who are gifted in this arena can immediately sit down at a computer and dance with it like they created the model themselves.

Not everyone is tech savvy, and if you are anything like me, you can get extremely frustrated when you don't have a clue about what you are supposed to do when a computer has glitches, unexpected virus popups, and unwanted ads. Sometimes a computer will even just crash.

The unexpected can cause you to just want to stop and quit! Shutting down, powering off, and feeling reluctant to reboot ever again. I feel the same way when I experience some people in my life who give me the flux. When the flow of our relationship begins to drive me down a winding trail. The only thing that puts me on "straight street" is remembering these relationships that are driving me crazy were not my idea, and I can go back to the creator and ask for help, the same way a person doesn't think twice of going to the manufacturer who created their computer.

Let's think about it. If you purchased a specific brand of computer, and it had problems, wouldn't you take your computer to the manufacturer of that specific brand to correct the issues? Well, I would hope that you would consider the one who created the computer as the best choice for fixing any issues that computer might have. The same applies to each of us when it comes to going to the correct source when we have issues with other people. The one who created us is the best option for fixing any problems.

Sometimes I must laugh when I think of the many relationships in my life that I have experienced. Relationships are truly God's plan because I have found myself saying these words out loud: "I *know* this was not my idea God!" I like to think God has a little chuckle with me in those moments. Yet, it is in these challenging relationships that I've grown the most.

No matter the circumstance, I know the only one who can fix, heal, mend, and design relationships is the People Expert. The Master of Creation, the one who knows all and sees us all, is the one we must turn to when we are experiencing brokenness in our relationships. God created and designed us for a purpose, and relationships help to reveal that purpose.

The turbulence of life will bring about relationships that sometimes can rock our boat. We can feel as if we are being left on a stormy sea, being tossed to and fro. We may feel as if the storm will never end. However, the good news is that there is a way out and that way is through Jesus. This may appear very dramatic, but that's why we are taking the time to examine our crazy relationships in life. If people are in your life for a season or a lifetime, there is a purpose. Even the ugly relationships that you wish would go away have a purpose.

One of the most important lessons to learn in life is, your relationship with God will be reflected in your relationship with others. It is my belief that God created us, and I believe that He is responsible for the creation of relationships. He understands them and how they should work in order to be successful. I have a relationship with God that I value and cherish. When my relationship with Him becomes stagnant or scarce, I realize my relationship with others is also going to be challenging. Understanding this has truly provoked me to stay as close to God as I possibly can. It is not an obligation or something I do by force. It is valuable to my life and the life I share with others to stay close to the one who created me. It is the love God has for me that has driven me to be healed in various areas of my life, repeatedly, relationship after crazy relationship.

This may sound like a simple choice, but you must know who God is to you personally in order for this to work. If you want your relationships to stop driving you crazy, you must know who to turn to, to have those issues fixed. You must know God. Do you know God? Are you confused in anyway about who He is and what role He plays in your life? If you answered yes to that last question, this is where you must start your journey on the road to being healed in your relationships.

Throughout my life I have been asked to simplify and prove who God is to me in my life, and who He should be to others or those who are asking this question. I can only speak to the way God centers Himself in my own life, but it is my hope that by doing that, the life I have lived so far will speak volumes as a testament to who He is to me. If you ask God to reveal Himself to you and ask Him to reveal Himself in your relationship with Him, then He will show up in all the areas of your life. He will NOT disappoint you. He will show Himself strong and mighty in your life if you ask Him. Perhaps you know Him already.

This would be a great time to discover the areas in your life that God wants to stretch you. Those areas of pushing you beyond your limits is where God takes the time to stretch you and mature you in your faith.

What area do you believe you need growth in your relationships? We all need people. We all need relationships, even when they drive us "crazy." All relationships have purpose, yes, even the perceived "crazy" ones.

Make a list of relationships in your life that are driving you crazy.

____

____

____

____

____

ᘏᘎ

Dear Heavenly Father,

Thank you for choosing me to have life with you. Thank you for my relationship with you which literally sometimes feels out of whack. My greatest desire is to become more intimate with you. I truly know that as our intimacy grows, my earthly relationships will be what you intended. I know that my relationship with you will affect my relationships with others. Thank you for choosing me, for loving me, and for giving me a blueprint of how to handle all relationships in my life so I can be a true reflection of you.

In Jesus' name, Amen

ᘏᘎ

"Love the Lord your God with all your heart and with all your soul and with all your strength and with all your mind; and love your neighbor as yourself." (Luke 10:27 NIV)

Reflections from my sister Shanna M Neal

I am the one small stair-step down sister of this author, Neesha Stringfellow. I can remember the years of our family relationships and being best friends. We depended on each other to show up at each major event in our lives to remind us that we were loved. I remember the first eighteen years of my life having my sister as the closest person in the world to me. After going away to school for four years and returning, I remember the first time I discovered there were a lot newer relationships in her life, and I was overwhelmed with them. One of my first thoughts was: How in the world can you be close to all these people at one time? I also thought to myself: Wow, how different my sister is from me in the world of relationships

One of those differences took time to deduce and distinguish was that I am a very "connecting" relationship person who loves and values one-on-one intimate connectivity. I do not like to travel in groups and gatherings of more than one or, at most, three other people. I enjoy focusing on one person at a time when going out to dinner or hanging out. My sister's relationship world felt like a revolving door of people in the middle of Michigan Avenue in downtown Chicago during the week of Christmas. If you've never experienced this, it's a door that is moving non-stop. This is what it felt like to be in my sister's relationship world. I simply couldn't keep up with all the names and levels of significance each one had in her life.

After years of observing this, I began to recognize the various compartments of her relationships were put into various categories like dresser drawers. The top drawers seemed to be filled with people that she called on daily for prayer, for information, and updates in the family life. The middle drawers were filled with people that were seen once or twice a week through activities like church, or business colleagues and clients. Then there were bottom drawers that seemed to be filled with lifelong relationships that weren't called upon as regularly but seemed to be like pillars in levels of respect and reverence. In all this sorting, there were still closets available for more formal relationships that sometimes-brought challenges, yet she knew that they were there for purpose. And finally, there was the attic where relationships were placed that were important at one time but are now a distant memory.

All the relationships have value and purpose. They bring out the best and worst in us so many times. I heard my favorite speaker and author, Dr. Myles Munroe, make a statement about relationships one day, "Don't make a brick a wall and don't confuse a wall for a brick when it comes to the people in your life." Everyone cannot be a wall, and we really wouldn't want to confuse those who are supposed to be more in our lives, like walls or pillars, with anything less. It is because of this principle that I appreciate and allow God to set the bar of who belongs where in my life. Will I place them in the top drawer where I need them every single day to either pray for or pray with? Will this be for a season or two that they are in the place?

In all our relating to one another, I've learned that it is important to let people know who they are to you and grant certain permissions. It is also important to identify those relationships that get to tell you your slip is hanging, you have something hanging from your nose, or your skirt is stuck in your underwear. If these very important relationships don't know that they have permission to tell you these things, then they probably won't. In many relationships, we sometimes assume that our closest friends should already know these things. In giving people permission to tell us that we stink, we are admitting that we will sometimes be wrong, or off, and we value the relationship enough to allow that person to be honest with us in these times. This reveals what kind of person and friend we are as well. Do we value honesty, confrontation, and transparency within any space in our relationships? These questions are not for every relationship we have whether family, friend, or foe. But our relationships say an awful lot about our character as well as who we will become.

As you sort through your top, middle, and bottom drawers, as well as your closets and attic of all the people in your life, you should remember that the friend you want to have is the person you first should work on becoming.

Chapter Two

Relationships: Whose Idea Was It Anyway?

It is my heart's desire for you to see how you can enjoy the different facets that make up every relationship in your life. One thing that won't go away in life is the people within it. It is key that we learn to navigate a healthy way of interacting peacefully with those in our circle of influence, even the complicated ones. Most of the time it's not that we don't like people, it's learning how to communicate and understand the purpose in our relationships, which will make a huge difference.

My own personal experiences in relationships have stemmed from those willing to walk with me through life at various stages. For example, some relationships continue with us always, while others are just for a season. They may walk with us while we experience stages such as childhood, teen years, our working years, as school friends, church members, counselors, and/or business associates. No matter how many people I talk to, I find that we can all find a commonality some place in our relationships. We can also find a teaching moment to reflect upon.

So, what's crazy about this book is it has encouraged me to continue to value and appreciate the people who are in my life already and the new ones I meet. My prayer is that it will inspire you to enjoy your good relationships, escape the ones which are not healthy, and give insightful purpose for even those complicated ones. Remember, relationships were God's idea.

"Relationships" are God's Idea!

In the beginning, God created a world that functioned well, until God created relationships, and then havoc because of relationships came about.

Listening to the bible story of Adam and Eve really infused me with anger as a little girl. I was so angry with Eve. Why did she listen to the serpent? Where was Adam? Why was she so intrigued with what the serpent offered her when she had it all? I laugh even as I write this question, because I guess our heavenly Father asks that same question regarding us. We are the King's kids, and He desires for us to know that we have it all. I can only imagine God asking us, "Why am I not enough? Don't you see me? I am your heavenly Father!" Over and over, and again I fail to pay attention to the love of God and my relationship with Him, which is the trump card that helps all relationships prosper.

Oh, the joys of relationships. Whose idea were they anyway? Ah yes! That's right! I believe it was the creator of life itself! God Almighty, Lord of Glory, the only true and wise living God! Yes, His idea. Because it was His idea, it would be awesome if all of mankind would recognize Him as the giver of life, not to mention desire to have a relationship with Him! Unfortunately, that's not the case. Instead, our creator of life gives us a choice to have a relationship with Him, and some have chosen not to seize that opportunity.

I was taught God's word as a little girl. I had to memorize scriptures weekly, sometimes daily. I repented of my sins and asked Jesus to come into my heart. The overwhelming presence of God filled my heart, and I knew He was real.

Relationships Are Still God's Idea!

It's so funny how I look back on it and remember crying my eyes out asking Him to fill me and to wash away my sins. The heart of that little six-year-old girl was so pure. I was not sure what I was asking, but it was sincere. I couldn't even begin to imagine the number of sins I had committed at that age; however, looking back on that moment, it is the purity of it that I long for even now. The genuine desire to be forgiven and to be in right relationship with the God who created me. At the age of six, I was declaring that I believed in God, and I knew I wanted to be His forever. I knew with all the pure desire I could fathom at that age that I loved Jesus.

Yes, I still love Jesus, but as you grow up, the world begins to desensitize your heart. Relationships must be cultivated, and a few distractions disguised as busy priorities can slowly cause the most important relationship in our lives to become cold, distant, or God forbid, forgotten. Saying the Apostle's creed kept the relationship I desired with my God front and center in my mind. I memorized it, and it wasn't long before the words became more than something I had to memorize. They became my declaration, a statement about what I believed identified the relationship that belief was (and still is) hinged upon.

I can honestly say at this age and stage of my life that I am still growing. I know I cannot live in this world without having the Almighty Creator, Father God, in my life. I allow life and busy to get me away from Him at times, but I still believe that without Him I can do nothing. I need to spend more time with Him! YES! The same desire I had at the age of six is the same today.

God has a purpose in it all; our relationship with Him will determine our relationship with others and will help navigate our relationships with others.

Although our journey in life is filled with many surprises, we must remember that all things work together for the good. Things will work out; God won't leave us alone even if we feel alone.

To know Him is to love Him, and to love Him is to live a life building and cultivating relationships with those He loves. I value my walk with Jesus. It is my desire that through every human relationship possible that I exemplify His love in my life and that He uses me to show the world how important it is to have a relationship with HIM! Life is worth the living because HE LIVES!

Write a letter to the heavenly father about your relationship:

____

____

____

____

____

ꕥ

Dear Heavenly Father,

I acknowledge that this entire relationship idea was yours, I also know that even through the craziest times in my life, it is my responsibility to lean and depend on you alone to remain healthy in all the relationships you have given me. I pray that you will continue to show me how to not withhold my feelings from you, but to return to you for guidance. Help me to remember that you can handle all and only you can teach me how to navigate each person in my life.

In Jesus' name, Amen

ꕥ

"He was in the world, and the world was made through him, yet the world did not know him. He came to his own, and his own people did not receive him. But to all who did receive him, who believed in his name, he gave the right to become children of God, who were born, not of blood nor of the will of the flesh nor of the will of man, but of God." (John 1:10-13 NIV)

Reflections from my sister Cynthia Means

Over my fifty-four years of life, I can say that God has taught me so many things about relationships, some I listened to and some I didn't.

Every relationship we have is God's idea, and I believe he gives us the tools to groom all our relationships according to our personalities.

Part of my personality has always wanted people to be happy and get along with each other no matter what. God has shown me that it's okay if there is some conflict, and it's not my responsibility to facilitate or manipulate anyone to keep peace. My responsibility is only to be intentional about showing love and concern, then I can trust God to do the rest.

I believe some relationships are hard on purpose to nudge us to our next level. Dealing with challenging relationships is especially hard for me, always being a peacemaker of sorts, but God's plan is always bigger than ours, and he sees the bigger picture that we do not see.

I have also learned that we must truly work at building a good community, because it won't just happen by itself. I believe some people are scared because of past experiences, and it causes them to withdraw from building connections with others.

We even teach little children starting preschool or Kindergarten to meet, greet, and hopefully be nice to the other children. This will introduce them to different personalities and help them understand cooperation at a young age.

As we get older and form different ideas and opinions, things tend to get a bit more challenging when it comes to relating to others. I have learned that people relate to others based on their life experiences, and some of those experiences may not have been great. Sometimes it takes a strong push, especially with family, to build the connections that God wants us to have, but we must cultivate each relationship on purpose. Every God encounter we have with other people will challenge us, push us, or nudge us in some way, but if our goal is love even in disagreements, we will all be changed for the better.

Chapter Three

Still Driving Me Crazy!

What type of relationship do you have with people? This is so important in order to have a healthy view of the areas we need to grow and mature. Some of the questions I ask myself may help you understand what areas the "crazy" shows up in life.

How would people identify you if they had to describe your relationship with them?

Have you ever wondered why people are in your life, and what purpose that they serve?

____

____

____

____

____

____

____

From the very beginning, God created man and said it is not good for man to be alone ... I am sure from the very start of Adam and Eve and the event of eating from the forbidden tree, man cried out, "Lord, this woman you gave me!"

If I am honest today, I find myself making the same statement, "Lord these relationships you gave me!"

Not every one of my relationships of course, but there are those times when turmoil or confusion or offense rise in a relationship, and I begin to feel like a victim and want to either bring resolve or cut people off.

We all know God places people in our lives for purposes and on purpose. Do we really have the clarity we need in order to maintain a great relationship? About the age of forty-five, more and more reflection began to flood my mind. I began to express gratitude for having an amazing life. I can truly say it has always been filled with great relationships. Challenges came from time to time, but I was always told to "keep living, things will change."

One of my heart's desires was to keep people in my life forever. I wanted my relationships to remain for a lifetime. I now know that this is not a realistic desire. I believe it came from never wanting to be abandoned, or never wanting to abandon people. My friendships grew and grew, new relationships would join the party year after year. What party? The party of my life, wanting everyone to come along. What was I thinking? People can't stay in your life forever. Life brings about growth and change. Well, it took me years to unfold that crazy idea of wanting every good thing to stay and remain in my life. When the some of my relationships began to be damaged, I quickly had to seek help from the brokenness that resulted. It was tough. There were relationships that came and then left, and sometimes I had no idea what went wrong. I know now that circumstances had shifted, and with that shift it brought about a change.

I allowed broken and closed relationships to take a toll on me emotionally. The cycle would repeat itself, where I would feel abandoned. I would then try anything and everything to fix the relationship.

Questions that filled my mind:

~ Who are you in my life?

~ Are you truly my friend or were you here just because you felt that there was a fringe benefit?

~ What can you do for me? What can I do for you? You scratch my back and I scratch yours.

- ~ Do you have manipulative and ulterior motives? Are you looking for something to gain? Eventually, it will all come out, so what is the true purpose of our relationship?

I can recall memories from early on that won't leave me and—yes! Guess what—they all involve people. The first relationship I admired was my maternal grandmother. My memory is vague, but I remember red beans and rice and cornbread on the stove along with French toast. Not a great combination; nonetheless, I remember her living in a nice quaint apartment in Hyde Park in Chicago. I recall I liked her style; I liked the way I felt going to her house. It was a sense of freedom and fun.

I can still hear my mom telling me how, at the age of three, and I told her I was running away from home because I didn't like being home, and she said, "Okay, stay here then." At the time it seemed like a great idea. The wonderful smell of Zestfully clean soap filled the air as I passed the bathroom, the fragrance of a place for everything and everything in its place was one of my heart's desires, crazy right?

At three years old, the relationship of who I thought my maternal grandmother to be was imprinted in my memory. My desire was to have the greatest relationship ever with her.

As time grew on and many years passed, my same grandmother, who I later discovered had many mental health struggles, came to live with me and my husband. I wanted her to come and stay with me because I still had the idea of my grandma being the one who rescued me at the age of three and taking me in when I wanted to run away. I loved having her there at my home. I enjoyed talking to her. She shared the stories of her three divorces, of her years of working and retirement, and of course her struggle raising her children, and so much more. I just knew I could help my grandmother with her state of mind.

Later, I had to come to terms with the fact that I could not help her. Only God could. So, what happened? My grandmother passed right in the middle of us having a very heated argument. This was one of the most painful experiences in my life. I thought it was my responsibility to make her feel loved, safe, and secure. It didn't matter to me that we were all stressed because our townhome was small. I only focused on helping her enjoy life and not focus so much on the past but look to the future. I just knew we had that kind of relationship. That was one big NOPE! I could not heal what was broken inside of my Gramma; I didn't realize that in a way I was making it worse.

I finally acknowledged that I needed to see the truth of what our relationship was, which was far from what I initially hoped it would be.

What was my intent and what was our relationship? I thought our relationship consisted of what I believe she needed and what she gave me, even during her own pain. Many years passed by where I continued to offer her hope. After my grandmother passed in my home I felt guilty and incredibly hurt for many years afterward, knowing that I would never have another opportunity to make it right with the one who'd made me feel so special. I coped by finding comfort in knowing that I found a special way to love her and understand her like no one else. I gave her the best I had to offer. I had to release her and realize I could not hold onto the pain of this lost relationship forever. The things I could hold on to were the memories we shared and acknowledge that God had fulfilled her purpose on earth and called her home.

Reflecting on my relationship with my grandmother helped me understand that from a very early age, I recognized that God gave me a gift for relationships. I also knew that all relationships would not always serve the same purpose. And I also realized that sadly, that not all relationships will be lasting relationships.

My gift of finding joy in relationships continued. It's funny how you struggle the most in areas that God will one day use those same areas to minister to others. During my early years I had become insecure in my relationships, be they friendships, family, church, business, work life, etc. As the years progressed, I felt like I became skillful in building relationships. However, there was a war within me that made me feel like I failed miserably in others. There have been so many connections throughout my fifty plus years of life, and I believe they have all had purpose. Life has certainly been a whirlwind of ups and downs, emotional trauma, and emotional healing. There was a time where I hid under a bushel of insecurity and false humility not owning my gift and purpose in life. Now, I even like to think that I have a PhD in relationships. Don't get me wrong, I am not saying I have it all figured out, or that I am an expert with all relationships. Absolutely not. I believe that through many of my own personal experiences, God has shed light on how relationships can be handled with love and care.

In this book, you will be able to read a few examples about the ups and downs of relationships from many walks of life. I am excited to share my journey with you and to allow you to embrace a different perspective. You can put a spin on your own journey in relationships as you go on this journey with me. Whether you are struggling with God our creator, or your job, your church, your friends, and family, or even yourself, take some time to really evaluate each relationship and look at it through a different lens. The goal is to make you laugh, smile, think, pray, and be determined to fight for the health and well-being of all of your relationships.

What relationships make you laugh, and smile?

ꙮ

Dear Heavenly Father,

I struggle with many of my relationships, to be honest some truly drive me crazy, I just wish some would go away, that others would just get right. Maybe it is me. Maybe I need to just get to the place that I put every relationship in your hands. Forgive me Jesus if there are areas, I need to do things different, and I haven't heard you. Give me an eye to see the areas where I have tried to have control. Lord Jesus, I place my heart and the heart of my loved ones at your feet. You have your way in my life.

In Jesus' name, Amen

ꙮ

"Do not be anxious about anything, but in everything by prayer and supplication with thanksgiving let your requests be made known to God." (Philippians 4:6 ESV)

"And we know that for those who love God all things work together for good, for those who are called according to his purpose." (Romans 8:28 ESV)

Reflections from my sister Rachel Jones

I grew up being the youngest girl of eight siblings, four girls, four boys. Neesha, the author of this book, was the oldest until we met an older sister, Cynthia. I had the awesome privilege of having a front row seat of watching my older siblings grow up and figure out life. I became a keen observer, doing what I was told, as I had many bosses, or moms and dads. I observed as they accomplished many victories, overcame various battles, and made small as well as huge mistakes. I saw my siblings court, date, become engaged, have break ups, get married, start families, and learn to raise their children. I had a front row seat in each of their lives, and what I did the most was observe and learn.

Although having a younger brother I was able to practice my bossy leadership skills, being the baby girl, I was still very much the baby. When I was seven years old, I went to my older brother Stephen (the preacher, ordained at 16), and I told him I wanted to accept Jesus into my heart and make Him Lord of my life. I hear so many stories of people who have accepted Christ over and over. That was not my story; I knew exactly what I was doing, and I was very serious about my decision. I accepted Christ then and forever, never changing my mind and turning away. That of course doesn't mean I never made mistakes; I made too many too many to count, and still do.

I grew close to the Lord early and continued to grow my relationship with Him daily. There is no height or depth in God, there is no end. We can always grow closer in our relationship with Christ. I learned a lot from my parents and siblings and church leaders on how to do this. Much I learned from observing and listening to people and at other times it was through being taught through scripture.

The most important thing I learned about relationships was that my relationship with Jesus had to be top priority and number one in my life. No other relationship could be more important than that. Not my mother, father, siblings, cousins, aunts, uncles, nieces, or nephews could take the most important place in my heart. Focused, and hungry for God, I made it a point to love Him with everything I had and make sure that no one, and no thing, came before Him.

This drive, focus, and sincere love for Christ gave me the desire to love what He loves and hate what He hates. God loves people. The greatest commandment Jesus gave was to love God with all your heart, mind, and strength, and to love your neighbor as yourself. My love for God became greater than my love for people and even for myself, and this gave me a deep love and compassion for people. People are the image bearers of God Himself, and He loves us all so furiously.

So, what has God taught me about relationships? He's taught me to care, to empathize, be compassionate, offer grace and mercy, the same things that I need. Along with that, in His word, God gave us all some tools to help, like "forgive quickly, be quick to hear, slow to speak and slow to get angry, don't be easily angered," and my favorite lesson in relationships is 1 Corinthians 13:4 NIV, *"Love is patient, love is kind. It does not envy, it does not boast, it is not proud. It does not dishonor others, it is not self-seeking, it is not easily angered, it keeps no record of wrongs. Love does not delight in evil but rejoices with the truth. It always protects, always trusts, always hopes, always perseveres"*

Love is the greatest way to win with relationships.

Now while all of what I said helps to keep the peace and make peace, it's not really detailed in the everyday conversations and intentionality that it takes to keep relationships healthy. Love, while it's the foundation for success, is a foundation we must build on with honesty, kindness, forgiveness, patience, and more. We must also know which relationships are for us and which ones are not. Some relationships I found to be seasonal, some for a lifetime, some were never meant to be no matter how hard I tried. Understanding this difference and allowing God to be the one to say who, what, and when is also very helpful. Prioritizing what God thinks about me, really helped me to rid myself of placing unrealistic expectations on people. It helped me to trust God with people and all their "crazy," including mine.

Honestly, I get relationships wrong a lot. To explain, it has a lot to do with the back story I began with. My birth order being the baby girl, as I said before, caused me to be shy, quiet, non-confrontational, and observant. I also had a lot of decisions made for me, making me a little terrible at being decisive. (My indecisiveness stands out most at restaurants.) Communication with others is not my strong suit. I learned of course along the way to make important decisions, confront, and stand up for myself when necessary. Now I am full of information and tools on how to make relationships great, but it is still a work in progress because I must be intentional, okay with conflict, and face it instead of turning away from it. I must speak up and talk it out, willing to resolve peacefully all that we have talked about. We must commit to do the work and allow love to be our motivation.

Chapter Four

Waiting on You

Well, I can honestly say my biggest struggle in the relationship game is wanting to see God change the people in your life who are not fully surrendered to God.

I had this experience with my husband. I wanted him to experience God in a real way. Like everything else in life, I needed his cooperation and partnership in this area of our lives also. We were partners in everything else and this couldn't be an exception, so I decided to stay home until he was ready. When I say stay home, I mean that I would stay home from traditional church services. I vowed to continue this routine until we could find a church, we both agreed upon so we could attend together.

How did that work for us? It did not work because neither one of us was looking whole-heartedly for the new church and place to worship God together. You can imagine how our individual relationships suffered with God and therefore with each other after a time.

I began to get into my comfort zone of saying, "Oh well, I will just chill and stay at home today," week after week.

I recall the first year and, might I add, the first of the three times I broke my ankle. I was sitting at home on a lovely little cream velvet loveseat.

I was sitting there nursing my ankle and not seeking that mutual place of worship for Wes and me. It was then I heard God speak to me.

I heard God say to me, "While you are waiting on Wes, I am waiting on you." It frightened me because no one was home except the babies and myself. I heard the voice so clearly, but I had not been in a consistently close enough relationship at that time to recognize the voice of my Father. After a moment, I knew it was my God, and I knew that He said what He said out of His love for me. It caused me to want to know Him more. I didn't want Him to have to wait for my attention, love, and devotion. I heard the voice for a second time, and I immediately called my aunt and asked her if she was willing to take me to a church I'd heard of in Chicago.

I acknowledged that God was going to take care of Wes, but He wanted me to know it was no excuse for me to sit on my do-nothing and wait for something magical to appear for my husband. There are many wives who go through frustrations with their husbands, hoping, wishing, and praying they will change, and I speak the same thing to them that God spoke to me, don't let God wait on you!

I mean it will drive you completely crazy thinking you can get a grown person to change. Waiting on them to shift.

I shake my head as I laugh about this today. I mean, did I think God would excuse me until my husband got himself together in my eyes? I really was crazy if I thought that. I learned that God's purposes and plans in my life needed to take place with or without my husband because if my personal relationship with God suffered, there would be no hope for Wes or me to have that happy and successful relationship I had dreamed of since I was a young girl.

Don't sit back and wait on people to change, pray for their surrender to God and not their surrender to you. We must take our control and place it at the feet of Jesus and realize it is not our responsibility to change people but to allow the love of God to change them.

In marriage, yes, you honor your husband and keep your home and family first, but don't let it stop you from worshiping and being obedient to the things God has called you to. God is a god of order, and he would not ask you or tell you to do something that would disrupt your relationship in your home. God is waiting on you. That's right, we often sit back and struggle with waiting on people, or for the timing of life to be perfect, or until we have enough money, or until, until, until. God is speaking to you and saying, while you are waiting on ... "I am waiting on you."

Let's stop making our heavenly Father wait. It will change everything if we just step into seeking His purposes and walk in the steps that are ordered by Him anyway.

What area in your life has God been waiting on you?

____

____

____

____

____

Dear Heavenly Father,

We often ignore your call because we are waiting on a certain turn of events to take place. Forgive us, dear Lord, for choosing to put you and the plans you have for us on hold. You deserve our surrender. You deserve us to trust you. We have been praying for a move in the lives of our husbands, wives, families, children, and so much more. Help me to realize if we lean and depend on you and only you, we will see you move on our behalf.

In Jesus' name, Amen

"May the Lord bless you and protect you. May the Lord smile on you and be gracious to you. May the Lord show you his favor and give you his peace." (Numbers 6:24-26 NLT)

Reflections by my sister-friend Brenda Baker

I have been a friendship kind of girl all my life. As a young person, I referred to every person in my life as my friend. Now as an adult, I still value friendships very much but understand the nurturing and investment they require. I reserve the label "friend" for those with similar values and beliefs, but also respect our differences.

One of Neesha's many superpowers is her God-given gift to make you feel like your place in her heart is just a little bigger than anyone else's. Regardless of your relationship, family, "framily," client, or customer, I'm sure everyone who knows her has experienced that special feeling at one time or another. She makes you feel seen, respected, valued, and loved.

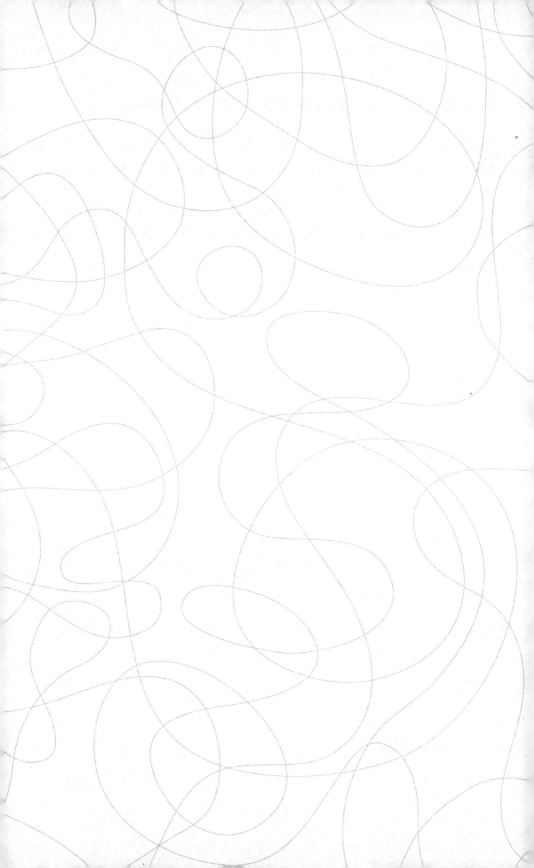

Chapter Five

Crazy Determination

The foundation of a relationship is so important. Even the very best of us have unforeseen circumstances that can create adverse effects and cause us to struggle in our relationships. We understand that nothing is perfect, and we will all make mistakes. The bible tells us we were all born into sin and shaped in iniquity. So, if you are looking for the perfect life, you won't find it until you get to heaven.

However, it is fair to have the determination to say 'yes' to embracing healthy behaviors and to take a stand and fight for what you believe in despite all the odds. You must start looking for the abundance of life on earth by seeking out counsel to be the healthiest person you can be and then allowing it to become contagious to those around you.

Every relationship will come with baggage and things we are not proud of, but God will take our story, and our baggage, and make it a testimony for His glory no matter how crazy it may seem or feel. We must trust and believe in His word and His promises.

I got married at the age of eighteen. I had a determination that, no matter what obstacles came my way, I was determined to figure out how to make the struggle of my beginnings turn out better than they began. More and more I began to create my own world, and over and over I made so many mistakes. Rather than asking God to lead my journey, my determination was to do it on my own. Of course, it was not intentional to leave God out of the picture, but sometimes we as God's people can become so determined, by any means necessary we want to look the part of having the "good life" rather than really making the necessary steps to walk that journey out with the grace of God and with authenticity.

Don't get me wrong, I would not change a thing about my humble beginnings. I did enjoy the journey of marriage and didn't just endure it. All the odds were against us. Statistics forecast that we would never make it to see the over thirty-four years of marriage we have shared. Our dependency had to become God first, then a strong family who stood with us. They encouraged us, not just with words, but with tangible support as well. We give honor and praise to Jesus for giving us the strength to love each other with His love, and then we truly thank God for family and friends who have stood by our side, especially through those early years.

My passion for seeing relationships healed was birthed out of the pain. I believe growing up in a home where there was not much peace. caused much of the pain. This was an area that I have prayed about often. Seeing families severed and divorced one by one over the years was heart breaking. I wanted to see healing in relationships, especially the ones God allowed me to have.

One by one, couples who were our friends began to get divorced. Many people might feel, *what does this have to do with me?* In my view it had a lot to do with Wes and I, for we saw ourselves as a community. I personally did everything in my power and strength to labor with our friends to convince them to stay together. To keep their relationships intact. Often I failed miserably because I was determined to do things in my strength. I learned immediately that God's plan was for me to practice Proverbs 3:5-6 and not just recite it.

We and all our friends began our marriages fighting for our families. Enjoying life together. Yet as young couples we did not realize the lingering pain that we brought into our marriages. Instead of just being determined to stay together, there had to be a determination to heal. Learning how to have determination to pray for our relationship and not control the relationships. Learning how to have crazy faith and believe that God is able to take you through any and all circumstances, not you. Grabbing hold of this concept was a real struggle for me over the years. I have not mastered it completely; however, I am determined now more than ever to lay every relationship at the feet of Jesus. I am more determined to lay every family member, person, marriage, child, church, and job at the altar and pray, "Jesus you see the crazy in many of these areas. I lay them at your feet. I trust that you will heal, mend the brokenness, and make us whole."

Did you see I used the word us? Yes, because it's never one-sided. Jesus wants to see me whole along with the people I am placing at His feet. He never disappoints. The pain of yesterday's bad experiences from past relationships, blended families, financial issues, not being able to fully provide for our families like we want to, can hurt us and our marriage.

Far too many people allow the world to define marriage and the family then wonder about the breakdown in our society. In order to see the true beauty in every relationship, share your story, share your determination for what you want to see, and take the necessary steps that will eliminate all the unhealthy influences and lead you to wholeness for yourself, your family, your children, your communities, and beyond.

It is my belief that most people do want to have healthy and happy relationships, and not just in a marriage. As with our physical body, there must be healthy choices made in order to live. The same is true with the spiritual. People need to put more work into finding the nutrition (reinforcement) that creates healthy families by focusing on those things that make for healthy relationships.

I would be remiss if I did not place in this book one of the most powerful messages, I heard by Pastor James Ryle over fifteen years ago. It stuck to my heart like it was branded and has never left me. I still embrace this and try to remember it when I become a little hard on those around me, realizing that we all grow at different stages in life. God's love for us allows us to grow and heal through every crazy cycle of life. We must be determined to go and to grow through them.

- Pastor James Ryle's Cycle of Life
- Healthy things grow.
- Growing things change.
- Changing things challenge.
- Challenge brings trust.
- Trust brings obedience.
- Obedience makes us healthy.
- Healthy things grow.

What areas are you determined to grow and heal?

ꕤ

Dear Heavenly Father,

Help us to have the faith and determination to never give up on ourselves and never give up on people. Please allow us to remember that you are ultimately in control, and without you we can do nothing. Help us to grow through every season with your love and your grace.

In Jesus' name, Amen

ꕤ

"But grow in the grace and knowledge of our Lord and Saviour Jesus Christ. To him [be] the glory both now and for ever. Amen" (2 Peter3:18 ASV)

Reflections from my aunt Pastor Miriam McFarland

Joy is what comes to mind when I think about the niece who first called me Auntie. That was a new relationship status I had never known before. I was only eight years old. I was so proud to be an aunt that I think I must have floated on air for the first few years after Neesha was born. She was the first one to call me Auntie Mimi. That's why I refer to her as my Number One. As my other nieces and nephews were added to the Crawford tribe, I was blessed beyond measure with an "aunt-hood" like none other. At least, that's how I view it.

As the years passed, life separated us by distance due to my college choice in Oklahoma and then my marriage, shortly after graduating. I didn't know what a long-distance aunt would look like, but I knew I didn't want to lose the bond I had developed with my nieces and nephews.

Because Neesha and I had that bond the longest, I figured our separation might provoke some deep emotions. She was only fourteen at the time.

I think she was mad at my husband, at first, as he was the one responsible for our nearly 1000-mile separation. It was a big adjustment for me as well. But it wasn't long before the love she had for me was shared with her uncle Bennie. They developed a special bond that was uniquely theirs. That's my Number One; she will find the path that leads to building meaningful, quality relationships even when her heart hurts.

A long-distance relationship was not something we would have chosen, but it was our reality. The dynamics of our relationship had to adjust, but I learned that being an engaged long-distance auntie was doable, if I was intentional about it.

There were not a lot of phone calls because, at the time, that was too expensive. So, I learned to appreciate USPS; my nieces wrote letters.

That was so gratifying, I felt so special when I'd open the mailbox and see a letter from one of my nieces (and on rare occasions my nephews).

Every trip home to Chicago was filled with making the most of family time. The main challenge was making that time last. We always seemed to need just a few more days together.

Fast-forward a few decades later, I can see the reward of being intentional in making the most of our time together. In the beginning, it was very hard for me to leave my big family in Chicago to move to Louisiana with my husband's family, which was small compared to mine.

The distance caused me to miss a lot of firsts in my nieces' and nephews' lives, but they were gracious enough to send me pictures. Back then, we didn't have cell phones or social media to stay in touch, but our relationships still found a way to thrive.

I learned that I should never take for granted small things like writing a letter, making a phone call, or in today's era, sending texts, sharing life on Marco Polo, Facetime, or whatever platforms we use.

Long-distance family relationships can have their challenges, but if we are determined to be intentionally connected with each other, every challenge is defeated. Strong family relationships, no matter how close or far the distance between us, are medicine for the soul.

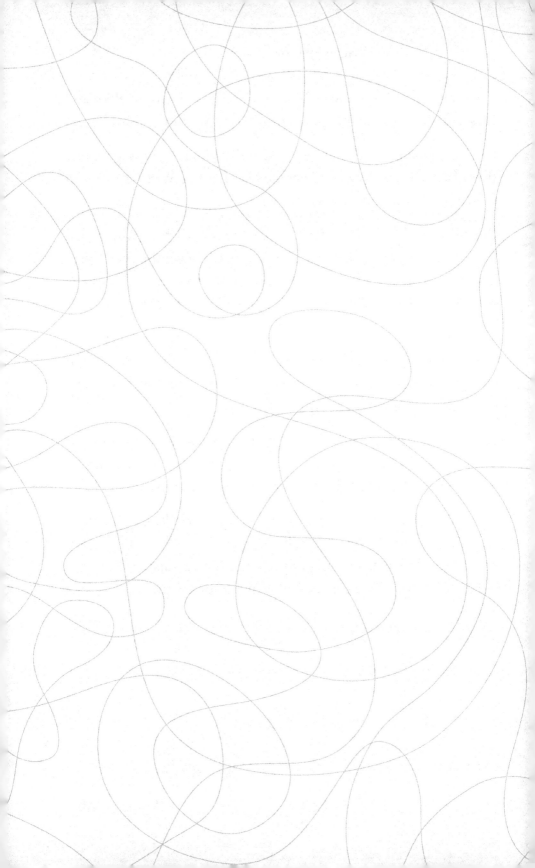

Chapter Six

Relationship Baggage

My Baggage. Your Baggage. Our Baggage!

There is a phrase that says, "Don't bring baggage from an ex-relationship into your next relationship, unless you want it to be a short trip." The author is unknown to me but the profound message behind that phrase is not lost on me. You can't talk about successful relationships without discussing the baggage that could potentially weigh you down and eventually sabotage your good intentions altogether.

- How do you deal with the baggage?
- Do you feel someone should "Take me as I am or have nothing at all!"
- Your baggage will draw repetitive relationships (when people ask the same questions, why do I keep attracting the same person.)
- Losing hope - too much baggage
- So many people lose hope after having so many bad experiences, or watching family and friends go through so much, until it feels the damage that has been done is totally unrepairable.

Hence the famous phrase: "I can do bad all by myself. No one wants to put up with the drama that comes with insecurity, unfaithfulness, comparisons, competitiveness, intimidation, and of course financial insecurity. In every relationship you are bound to have one or more of the things listed. But how do we cope or live with them when you are in so deep? Both parties must be willing to go to counseling and to receive suggestions.

Relationship Counseling Should Be Mandatory!

Self-repair is the best way to make sure you don't always look for the fault in another person. Make sure you examine and see if you find any areas that you could use some self-repair from your creator. Find out the things that are not in complete working order. What areas do you need a checkup or possibly need to get a prescription from the Master Physician?

Do you always see what's wrong with the other person? Do you need to examine yourself spiritually? Let me answer that for you. Yes! We all need this self-examination of ourselves from time to time. We are never past the stage of growing and learning to be better, communicating better, and showing that growth to the ones we are in relationships with. True relationships require intimacy and trust. Trust allows those in a relationship to not only support each other spiritually, physically, and mentally, but also financially. Women and men both must feel some sort of support from the other partner. It has nothing to do with the actual finances coming into the relationship as much as what is done with whatever comes into the household. This goes back to intimacy and communication as well. If you invest in anything, consider investing in Godly counsel and relationship and/or life coaching as it pertains to the different relationships in your life but especially to your marriage.

SINGLES and SATISFACTION

The single relationship can appear to be carefree and filled with joy and excitement. For others it can be difficult and frustrating, especially for those who desire to be married.

I remember the phrase from the words of Eddie Murphy on *Saturday Night Live, "Lookin' for love in all the wrong places..."*

Well, it appears to be one of the hardest tasks in life to find the one, the right one. Of course, statistics tell us that women outnumber men, and especially good men. Rumor has it that women come with more baggage than men want to deal with. I don't quite understand how all this works, especially since I have not had to date, or ever live as a single woman. However, I've done some research and found some simple things singles should know.

Groundbreaking Conversations to Promote Healthy Relationships

"Dating without the intent of getting married is like going to the grocery store with no money. You either leave unsatisfied or you take something that isn't yours."—Jefferson Bethke

Living Single. Realistically, what does this really mean? I just don't believe people start out as children and never dream of being in a relationship. Who really wants to live single? There might be some exceptions to the rule, but basically everyone desires to love someone, to have a person to do life with, to enjoy the comfort of sharing the warmth of a bed. It's human nature. I believe God designed us to want companionship. God's word does state that that man should not be alone.

I have been asked the question repeatedly, "Then why are so many people single?" I think people really want me to have the answer, but I don't have that answer.

I've heard so many mixed reviews about being single. Do you remember the television show in the nineties, *Living Single*? The show centered on the lives of six friends who shared personal and professional experiences while living in a Brooklyn brownstone. Now I must say their lifestyle was somewhat realistic in some ways, and in other ways it was a joke. Today as we look at the single lifestyle, the world has identified it so differently. Today's idea is that being single should not keep you from doing anything you want to do, so marriage isn't really necessary.

What Do I Do While I'm Waiting?

Enjoying life while you are waiting is the main thing, I believe is important. Sometimes people are ready to jump into a relationship, but they are not quite sure what they really desire themselves. It's so important to have a vision. A vision to know the truth about yourself and your goals. Learning how to love yourself and be content. Learning how to seek God for your desires and not seek after them yourself. Having a desire to be healed from the baggage of the past no matter what that baggage is. Seeking out wise counsel to help you mature while you are waiting on the gift of a relationship is also important.

What is the one thing you should not put up with while dating? Think about this question seriously. You need to know the boundaries and limitations up front, so you won't allow someone to push a line that you don't want crossed. Write your boundaries down. It is also a good idea to get the help of others when seeking answers to the kinds of issues that might come up with dating.

Me, you and who? Exclusive or inclusive? Know the differences. Be smart when it comes to how you spend your time and with who you spend your time with. The saying is true that who you include in your relationships and who you find in your circle of influence will impact the end results. Settling brings pain and heartache. This isn't the kind of settling like someone moving into a new place and settling into new surroundings. This isn't the kind of settling that speaks to your comfort. This type of settling is the kind when you take what is in front of you because you lack patience. You are not willing to wait for the right relationship, so you go for the relationship in front of you right now.

The second issue may be that you may feel pressured by outside influences for one reason or another. Therefore, having a relationship with God, the Father is crucial. When we settle for less than God's best, it can lead to pain for more than just the couple. As fingers are being pointed at who is to blame, it can cause a lot of hurt. Some of those hurts can take a long time to recover from, increasing the potential for baggage to be carried over into a new relationship in the future or even the current one. There is no one that knows who is more perfect for you than your heavenly father. There is an art to avoid settling and it depends on being close in relationship with God and listening to the plans that He has for you, and those plans include plans to prosper you in your relationships.

Remember: If you don't love yourself, you won't know how to love someone else the way they deserve to be loved.

Strength Assessment

Consider the following. Take time to think about your answers and overall thoughts regarding each:

- I am happy with my life alone.
- I don't have baggage and I'm not carrying forgiveness.
- I know what it means to love myself.
- I know what it means to love others. I trust people.
- I can see the good in others before I see the bad.
- I know how to become satisfied with the life I'm living before marriage and a full commitment.
- I have discovered what I love for myself. Hobbies and talents—I am learning to love what I like to do while single.
- I am fulfilled with being single; I feel whole and complete. I know no one is perfect, but I should know you and like you before our relationship begins.

So, I Meet Someone! We Start Dating, Now What?

So, what are the rules of dating? There are countless books that have been written that we can read. I happen to believe the following:

- Write the vision of what you desire in a mate.
- Write down non-negotiables even though they might change.
- Relationships should not dictate what you want, you cannot control everything.
- Set boundaries.
- Needing Space or Growing Apart.
- Standards—what are they? Only you know.
- Alone is not lonely, get to know yourself.
- Can you enjoy yourself alone?

These are all questions I encourage people to ask themselves before diving into the commitment of marriage. Marriage is indeed a gift but you need to know who you are before marriage.

College kids usually learn how to adapt alone before they go to college. However, if you don't know how, you get a crash course when you go. Being alone does not mean you have to be lonely. There is a common stereotype that being by yourself means you are lonely. Having relationships with friends who are single and satisfied has given me much insight into the peace you can have while you are waiting on the love of your life to come along.

My personal belief is that God did not intend for man to be alone, He states it in His word. I believe God's word, but I also realize that man has a choice. My prayer for those who are single and satisfied, or single and waiting for God to bless them with a mate, is that you love yourself, know what you desire, work on receiving healing in the areas you personally need it, and live life to the fullest and wait on no one.

ഗ്ര

> Dear Heavenly Father,
>
> Bless me as I am waiting on you to reveal your purposes and plans for my life. Help me to never feel alone, but always experience your joy in the season of being single. Give me the desires of our heart. Help me to remember I am never alone.
>
> In Jesus' name, Amen.

ഗ്ര

"Beloved, I wish above all things that thou mayest prosper and be in health, even as thy soul prospereth." (3 John 2 KJV)

Reflections by my sister-friend Carla Mosley

Relationships have taught me to allow people to be who they truly are. Let them reveal themselves to me naturally, and then I can decide if who they are is "enough" for me. With all the relationships I have experienced in my lifetime, I have realized that I cannot control the outcome of other people's expectations of me. But I can challenge myself to control the way that I respond to my relationships, and that is where I find my power.

Chapter Seven

Marriage and Other Relationship Ideas

Marriage

One of the greatest gifts when it comes to relationships is marriage. Did you know that marriage was God's idea also? God designed the family, and within that family are relationships that successfully help us live and cooperate in worshiping and giving thanks to the God whose idea it was to bring us into existence.

I recall that at the very beginning of my marriage I made two declarations. The first thing I declared and determined in my heart was this: that I was going to be happy. The second thing that I declared was that my marriage was going to be an example of a successful relationship. It was crazy; we were so young and married sooner than we planned as our first child was on the way.

From the very beginning, I recognized that God's hand was on our marriage. I thought for the most part we had everything under control, *yet* something in me knew that it was going to take me partnering with God in order to achieve my true relationship goals.

Many people spoke negative words over our marriage, saying we would not make it through the first five years. After we reached those five years, I am proud to say we were still happy. We then heard about the "seven-year itch" wondering if there would be any changes to our gifted union. We were still happy after seven years. By the time we got to twenty years, we were warned that most couples, if they were still together, learned to tolerate each other for the sake of the children, drifting into a kind of complacency. We did not allow fear to grip us, and yes there were challenges; however, we chose to face them together rather than disconnect from each other. Now we have just celebrated our thirty-fourth year of marriage—we are still happy and still learning and growing together.

The famous James Brown wrote a song, "It's Cheaper to Keep Her." During those rare times when we would have a quarrel, I would say to Wes, "Well, just divorce me then." His comment would always be, "It's cheaper to keep you," sometimes causing us to continue to argue. But eventually, over time, we learned to laugh. We realized that our love was stronger than any obstacle we faced, and our commitment to maintaining a loving relationship was even stronger.

Marriage and Other Relationship Ideas

Encouragement from others played a major part in our love remaining strong. Finding a good support system for any relationship is crucial. We attend marriage retreats, workshops, and receive counseling, and it all speaks to the commitment a husband and wife must have for the relationship to be healthy. Our daily peace and joy are maintained by how well we keep our heavenly connection. The relationship between a man and woman was God's idea, and that includes marriage.

We must keep our relationship with the creator strong so that every intricate detail of our lives will be strong.

The greatest deception that our generation has bought into is that we can make it on our own. No matter how well we appear to be taking care of ourselves, our very next breath and moves are dependent upon the grace of our heavenly Father. If we trust Him, He will never fail us or let us down. As mere men and women we may not understand the paths we have to journey in our marriage, but if we recognize how we are not in it alone, we can have joy throughout our journey, no matter what it brings.

Two really are better than one. Remember that no matter how crazy things can get in your relationship in marriage, you and your mate, and you and your heavenly Father, are walking down the path as He guides you into true intimacy in your covenant relationship with Him and in your covenant relationship with your spouse. The scripture below is a good reminder how important covenant relationships really are.

"It's better to have a partner than go it alone. Share the work, share the wealth. And if one falls, the other helps, but if there's no one to help, tough! Two in a bed warm each other. Alone, you shiver all night. By yourself you're unprotected. With a friend you can face the worst. Can you round up a third? A three-stranded rope isn't easily snapped." (Ecclesiastes 4:9-12 MSG)

Neither of you must ever feel alone. *There is someone walking with both of you.* You are not solely dependent on yourselves for the success of your relationships. By grasping this truth, you will see the difference in every area of your life! Remember that God is here to help because relationships are His idea.

"Let us hold firmly to the hope that we have confessed, because we can trust God to do what He promised..." (Hebrews 10:23 KJV)

ഌൻ

Dear Heavenly Father,

Help us to know that you are the reason marriages can work. You designed marriage. Oftentimes it feels as though we are walking through life alone in our marriage, but we must lean and depend on you to carry us through. I pray for joy, peace, and laughter in every marriage. Thank you for the opportunity and the gift of marriage. Let our marriage reflect your love for us.

In Jesus' name, Amen

ഌൻ

Reflections by my daughter-in-love Kelani Timaul

Being married in our early twenties, me at twenty-two and Gevon at twenty-three, we were still figuring ourselves out as individuals. Not being our complete selves as an individual meant we were also finding out who we were as a couple. It came with lots of work, uncomfortable conversations, prayer, and growth. If there's one thing I'd have to talk about when it comes to what I have learned in a relationship/marriage, it would be to never stop learning. Twelve years later, we have changed as a couple and as individuals. We have learned and re-taught each other countless amounts of times throughout these years, and it's been an adventure the whole way.

Change is constant, and marriage isn't an exception to this rule. What change does in a relationship is allow for learning opportunities. After so many years of marriage, it's easy to think we can't know anything more about a person, but then you learn something new: a simple conversation to learn a childhood memory you realize you haven't heard before or paying attention to the fact they now eat a certain food that they wouldn't have eaten before. These seem minuscule, but the broader picture is the fact that we continue to learn who our spouse is and continue to choose to love them wholeheartedly. Marriage is spending a lifetime of learning together. Make sure those lessons are worth it.

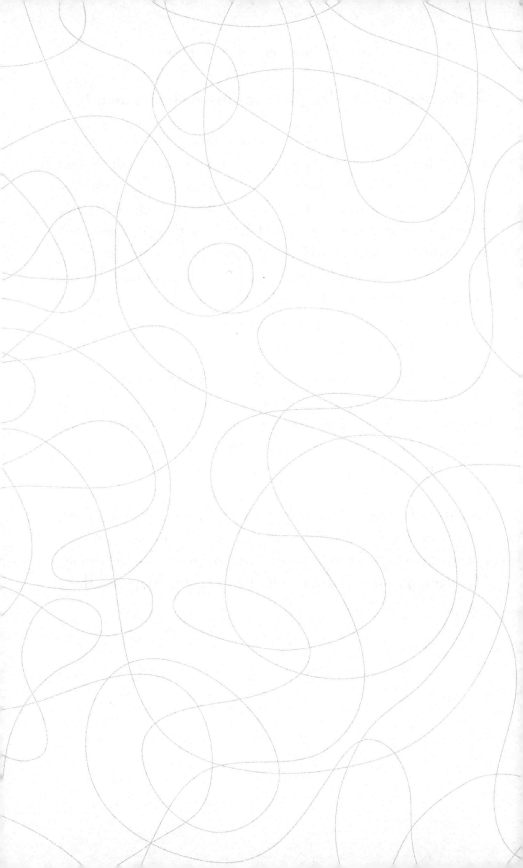

Chapter Eight

Rescue Me!

After years of coaching and counseling hundreds of couples, I realize that many of the relationships were founded upon a rescue mission. The hope that couples would fall in love instead of needing rescue would be ideal. However, when the rescue mission is over and life takes a different turn, and people find out what they really want in life, unfortunately problems arise, and couples tend to state that the spouse is not giving what it is that they desire. This is something that can happen even when each individual person was rescued by their significant other.

Oftentimes, relationships are built on empty voids that people have in their lives. So, coming to the rescue, helping someone out or encouraging someone, like rescuing a damsel in distress, will allow you to temporarily put off the emptiness and cover up the roots of what's going on in your own personal journey. It doesn't mean that you can't help someone while you are getting help yourself, but it does mean that there is a possibility that you can unknowingly use someone to ignore what's really going on inside of you. This will bring on future unwanted stress and pain in a relationship. It's important to know what each relationship was built upon. Do I really know a person, or did they rescue me and come into my life in a season where there was so much neediness that I embraced them? God can do work in every relationship, but it's still vital to make sure you know who you are as a person. Sometimes you can be the rescuer, or you can be the one who is rescued. I have been both, and I learned very quickly that this great relationship or friendship that I thought I had and that was so solid was built on a fleeting circumstance and not true authenticity. It was instead built on a need.

The biggest assumption that people make is to assume that because we are in a relationship that I can automatically read your mind; everybody has a different perspective and a different way of thinking and hearing.

The giver often expects a person to receive automatic information in knowing what people mean. Your past hurt and pain is like honey that has stickiness from your past. Heal from the past and the present won't be so heavy and hold you down. Healing unlocks the handicapped potential that has been in prison and wants to be free in every relationship.

Now, I am no expert on the subject, but having had the opportunity to have been a hair designer for the past thirty years as allowed me to encounter all types of people. One of the phrases or statements I make all the time is: you attract people like yourself. People have all sorts of drama and life experiences. They also have their own idea of what they want in this life. It is not until you build a relationship with a person that you are introduced to intimate parts of their life, and they with yours. However, sometimes people don't want to share their innermost feelings with someone else until they feel safe. This can cause a problem in the relationship.

Having the ability to share intimate details is one of the keys to building a good relationship. When we have an open relationship, it is because we feel as if we have the freedom in the relationship to share.

When something or someone draws you into a conversation, it's the beginning of an opportunity to allow people into your space. A simple attraction can start with a compliment, or a word of compassion, or a feeling of empathy to show where you have some of the same things in common. I can speak from experience.

Allow me to expound on this thought. My obsession with shoes draws me to notice anyone and everyone's shoes when I enter a room. It is usually a conversation starter when I take courage and open my mouth to speak and say, "I really like your shoes." The courage comes from the different experiences I have had with shoes. From an early age, I had trouble with my feet and had to wear orthopedic shoes. From the age of ten, I suffered with ingrown toenails and hated my feet and my toes. I decided early in life I would always have amazing shoes. I noticed shoes with envy, everywhere, from the time I was a little girl, and my desire to have pretty shoes only became stronger the older I became.

Being polite about complementing people's shoes is far from my point; however, it is an example of how connecting my journey, my story, gave me an introduction with a new person, like starting with a simple compliment, and allowing that to grow into a new relationship. If a person reciprocates being transparent, it may allow them to find out the other story behind my obsession with shoes.

Authenticity, real conversations, and real talk allow people to be open and know if it's an open door for building a relationship.

People are constantly assessing if they want to be or stay in a relationship with us. I've had to answer the "me, myself, and I" questions on multiple occasions. Some questions I failed to answer appropriately, but I have learned from my past experiences and concluded that I needed to first interview myself. One of the reasons I take the time to do this was because if I expect others to respect me and have a great relationship, I need to know who I am, what I desire, and in what areas I need to grow.

I want to share some of the questions and answers with you that I ask myself.

Transparency

Q: Who am I?

A: I am a nice person, friendly, exciting, fun, serious at times, creative, intense.

Q: What is my purpose?

A: To encourage, love, pray, live to the fullest, grow, change, exhort, smile, laugh.

Q: Where can I be effective?

A: In my home, community, church, job, anywhere where there are people.

Q: Where do I need to grow?

A: Heal, hurt; forgive quickly; stop being lazy at times; slow down, say no more often; smell the roses; not be angry with myself for incomplete tasks, not compare myself to others and their accomplishments. Stay focused.

Q: How can I help?

A: Use my gift, be confident in my calling, enjoy the beauty in others and not focus on the negative, believe for someone until they can believe for themselves.

Q: When did things change?

A: At the ages of thirty, forty, and now almost fifty, when I experienced grief and loss.

Q: When did I change?

A: Changed when I acknowledged I needed it for my future, to experience growth, when I yielded to becoming more of a student intent on learning.

Q: Why?

A: I am because God says I am, I will because I can see, I won't because I have discipline, I say yes because it is my purpose.

Q: How can I change?

A: Receiving the love of God and allowing Him to change me. Yielding to the spirit and not to my flesh. Willing to shift when the seasons change. Respecting that people change and nothing is forever except the true Love of God!

These are truly questions I had to begin to look at and then answer. I don't get it right all the time, but in order to have healthy relationships, these questions are vital to my own well-being, and to others.

Now I would like to encourage you to answer these very same questions for yourselves. Don't skip this part of the book. Believe me, you will be missing out on finding some meaningful answers that God has been waiting on you to receive. Admitting to the areas I needed growth in relation to myself allowed me to know and understand myself and others even more, and I believe answering these questions will do the same for you.

How do I expect others to understand what I desire from a relationship if I don't really know myself? The reflection of being honest with myself and asking myself some questions helped me tremendously.

After this reflection you may find yourself at the feet of Jesus and that is a great place to be.

Some of the most encouraging benefits have been watching people change and seek more for their life. Personally, I have learned so much throughout the years that has challenged me to know that every wise person needs counseling. The best counselors need counseling, just like the best teachers need a teacher.

Never stop seeking wisdom about life and your relationships. Recognize there are seasons, reasons, and lifetimes where some people are there and other times when they are not. Some people are meant to be a post and some a pillar. Posts are there for the season of building the foundation. Pillars are there for the duration of the house, helping it to keep standing. See people for the position where they are, not where you want them to be, and then give them space to work out their life in the positions they are called to.

Dr. Myles Munroe's declared what has become a famous quote, "Where there is no purpose, abuse is inevitable." Beware and be watchful that you have purpose and are living it out daily.

I have learned to respond differently to the various life experiences I've had. I believe how you respond to a thing determines your outcome. My responses have not always resulted in the best outcomes, but I have learned from my choices and now I will make better ones in those moments where I can live out what I've learned.

A saying in Proverbs brings this phrase to mind, *"A word fitly spoken is life apples of Gold in pictures of silver."* A word fitly spoken is like apples of gold in settings of silver.

Asking the right questions is crucial in a relationship. Understanding and taking ownership for weaknesses will help us to get through weak moments and build strength for future relationships. Admitting when you need to try a different approach and sharing the desire to grow with those you love has the power to make all the difference. You need them to know you have a genuine desire to change because you want the relationship to work. It really isn't about the other person as much as it is about each of us individually. Be willing to see help immediately if you discover a consistent pattern of experiencing chaos in a multitude of your relationships. Do you ever feel like you want to grow, and it appears that everything is at a standstill?

Do you experience feeling like you are not happy with the relationship and then you're asking yourself: why am I here? If those thoughts arise, seek help. You are not the only one asking that question.

Operating in faith and not fear is the first step. Fear keeps you handicapped or in a position of vulnerability to your enemy's plans for you. You will never be able to move forward when you are paralyzed by fear. First of all, everyone is not out to get you, and sometimes, previous hurt causes us to have our guard up when a guard isn't necessary anymore. Some people think everyone wants something from them but that is simply not true. The truth is to learn what is necessary for the different dynamics and experiences in new relationships.

It is true everyone does not have your best interests at heart, but you are not going to encounter everyone in your lifetime. You will encounter some that either need the opportunity to be fitted in or to be removed from your life. You will come across people who have manipulative and ulterior motives in trying to gain your trust and friendship. When you discover this, surround yourself with wise counsel and go on with your life. The ones that have a negative intent toward you will eventually be found out and dealt with as you learn to trust God. God knows your heart; you have to trust Him with each and every person who comes into your life. Proverbs 4:23 tells us to guard our hearts with all diligence for out of it flows the issues of life.

Guarding your heart does not mean having a closed mind to people because of fear of hurt. I am reminded of the Bible message of Judas Iscariot, the disciple who betrayed Jesus. I am sure that Jesus was hurt when Judas betrayed Him, but he fulfilled a purpose. Oftentimes, people are in your life to assist you, and yet they only find ways to assist themselves in what they can gain from you. The trust factor is revealed when you jump all in and trust that God is the Keeper of your heart. He will lead and guide you into all truth. Is that possible? Yes, it is possible to be transparent. It is impossible to say you will never experience hurt. However, if we experience hurt, it is for our own good and we must trust the process. We will come out victoriously. It goes back to how we respond to every circumstance of life. Does that mean that sometimes things won't catch us off guard and blindside us? No, it does not, it just means everything, and I mean everything, should be preceded with prayer, and lived out in prayer.

Blind Spots

We all have blind spots, some more than others. Some people can't see the truth because they have been living in a mode of self-defense for so long that self-defense becomes common. It is natural to protect yourself when you see or feel danger coming. The unfortunate thing is that we are the same way with our relationships. If we have been hurt in the past, it is natural to want to build up defense mechanisms to make sure we don't get hurt again. I am not sure if we are not aware of warning signs, or that we just don't listen or pay attention to the signs. We sometimes plunge into a relationship and don't think to look out for how we should handle each area of our relationships. We put up "blind spots."

So, What About the Healed Me?

The journey has been long, but it will be ongoing forever. I take pride in knowing that even if I have not learned everything in this life about my relationship with myself, I have learned that *I must heal.* I will constantly be looking for, seeking, and praying for guidance to know the only way for me to be the healthiest person in life, to be the authentic Me, Myself and I begins with recognizing that as long as there is breath in my body, there will always be another opportunity to continue on a road that leads to healing. Every season will present another journey of healing. No matter where you are, who you are, always ask yourself the question, *how am I doing?* Checking in on "you" will continue to help you be the healthiest you there are, and every relationship you will have throughout your life will only improve.

ℬ

Dear Heavenly Father,

I realize I have been guilty of taking your place in many of the relationships in my life, from family to friends and beyond. Please forgive me for being the rescuer in other peoples' lives and forgive me for having an expectation of being rescued by someone who is close to me. I am asking to lean and depend totally upon you alone, relying on your word to keep me grounded.

In Jesus' name, Amen

"Casting the whole of your care all your anxieties, all your worries, all your concerns, once and for all on Him, for He cares for you affectionately and cares about you watchfully." (I Peter 5:7 AMPC)

Reflections from my cousin Raquel M. Robvais, PhD

Relationships. My favorite book in the bible is Ephesians. It is the magnum opus of Paul's writings, as he sings the praises of God's grace. For after all, everything begins with grace, moves through it, and finishes up because of it. This indispensable gift, this spiritual endowment, is always previous and present; it bookends our days, weeks, months, and years. With grace, we get a glimpse into the love of God, why He thought about us before the world became a habitable place. With grace, we peer into the plan devised to demolish the wall of sin that separated us from Him.

Ephesians explains who we are in Christ and what that really means; it tells us that because we are in Him, we have a seat far above powers, principalities, and rulers—the entities that we stand against and sit above. The devil is defeated—not all powerful, not all knowing—he's not greater but smaller, not victorious but a victim of the cross, the grave, and the blood.

Sandwiched in between the articulations of victory over the enemy and our identity with Christ are admonitions of how we put these grandiose truths to work in the pedestrian journey we call life. For that, we need grace. To be sure, Chapters 1-3 give us our equipment to live with, and Chapters 4-6 tell us where we use this equipment, how to operate the equipment, and why it's necessary. More specifically, the spiritual blessings, the hope of our calling, the knowledge of His love, and the special seat with Christ are useful to have good relationships, to live with each other, to grow in His character, and to be salt and light to our world.

In these chapters, we get a sense that the folk reading the original text are no different than those of us who amble about in churches, synagogues, and other places of worship. They loved God but had trouble on occasion loving each other. They had challenges with relationships. We do too. According to Merriam Webster, relationship is defined as "the state of being related or interrelated, kinship, a state of affairs existing between those having relations or dealings." It's a partnership, a union, a collaboration. These dealings that we have with each other are often reflections of what we have with ourselves, of how we are on the inside. We don't know how to get along with others until we know how to get along with ourselves. We must learn that, as a Christian, Christ makes us good, makes us valuable, makes us honorable. And that's enough, always. This settles the restlessness in my soul and stills the need to work to please and to get approval from others. This also requires that I remember others are going through the same process, the same learning and knowing. It requires that I remember grace, for them in the journey, and grace, for me to understand their voyage.

Grace is our teacher and our toolkit. I know this in a particular way. Grace teaches me how to live without my mother; going to heaven was her idea, not mine. When I want to get disgusted with her for leaving, Holy Spirit reminds me to give her grace, allowing her the freedom to choose, and being okay with it. We never fully mature and figure relationships out; that's what our adventure with Holy Spirit is about. He teaches us how to love ourselves and to love each other. His instructions seem monotonous and rather tedious: put off and put on; stop telling lies, tell the truth; quit stealing, use your hands for work; don't use abusive language, let everything you say be good and helpful; get rid of bitterness, rage, and anger; be kind, tenderhearted, and forgiving; don't be greedy, be thankful; husbands, love your wives; wives, adapt to your husbands; children, honor them both.

Replacing the put offs with the put ons is the starting material and sustenance for solid relationships. Twenty years of marriage has schooled me in putting off and putting on; surprisingly, these lessons have been more for me and not so much for my husband. I've learned that putting off independence is an intentional act when adapting to my husband is not so appealing. I've learned that putting off having the last word in an argument is just as sexy and attractive as putting on lingerie or anything else he loves.

Having a relationship with two teenage daughters requires that I put off lying, living under the guise that I really do know what's best all the time. And instead put on submission, listening to their unique voices, learning their unique ways, and living with them according to the grace God has given. Ultimately, putting on says they are His and not mine, and He knows what's best.

Without the put offs, we are miserable misfits living in a "world of illusions." Without the put offs, we lose our saltiness and dim our light. And the world we inhabit continues to live hopelessly confused. To be sure, we can't stop lying on our own, we can't do good to our enemies, and we can't love our neighbors or change our behavior without the gift of grace. Every relationship is infused with grace when it's successful, and every relationship is empty of grace when it's not. Grace reveals His love for us and how we should live with one another. This is a journey, an adventure with God to cultivate the kind of relationships that "brings out the God-flavors of this earth, bringing out the God-colors in the world."

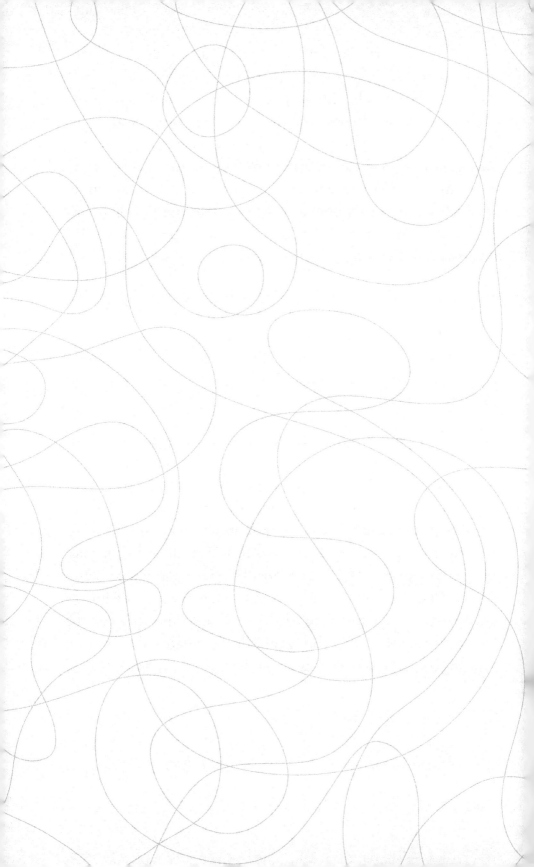

Chapter Nine

Reboot Your Relationships

My belief is simple, yet effective: you cannot move forward in life without the understanding that people and relationships were God's idea. It requires trusting Him. No matter what, you must be self-aware, or better yet "spirit aware.". Does this mean walking around with a detection radar every day? NO! It just means relaxing and trusting the one who created these relationships.

It is important to remember, when dealing with transparency in relationships, that we are speaking to those who know without a shadow of a doubt their point of view regarding the relationship. The belief that there is purpose in being connected with this person. This idea of "dealing" with people is not the best interpretation of the word. Dealing with people in my opinion is like a job; instead, we should be growing with people. The more we are in relationship together with anyone, it should be a growth experience for both of us.\

Ask yourself the question: what is it like being connected to me? We should be self-aware regarding what others might gain while being in relationship with us. I have stated this often, relationships are never one-sided, and it's imperative that we are reminded of what others gain from being connected to us as well as what we receive. Are we healthy? Are we secure?

I have failed repeatedly, and even gone into a pity party at many moments in my life where I would be frustrated with others and didn't realize I needed to take a step back and check myself, taking some time to think about where I can improve in the relationship.

I ask myself the question: Do you care about what others think about you? We must ask ourselves: Where do I need improvement? People don't tend to do that one simple thing. We don't do a self-check on a regular basis. Instead, we have a tendency of looking at how others are treating us or how they are responding to us in our relationships.

How can we stop and make those types of assessments and ask those type of questions?

Give yourself a strength assessment. Ask the questions: How strong are you? What type of background did you come from? Do you have many relationships, friendships? Do you find yourself having a fall out with people, or people misunderstanding you most of the time? What type of friend would people say you are? Reflecting on the fact that God said Man should not be alone definitely demonstrates that He created relationships. God chose to have it this way. When you understand who you are, whose you are, and what you were created for, it sets you up for success in life and relationships.

My husband and I wrote a book called *Reboot your Marriage*. As we have taught from this book for almost ten years, I often tell people truly the book can be used for more than marriage. I have read it repeatedly and come to terms with rebooting my own crazy.

The *Reboot* series mentions how every person in life needs a refreshing, or a realignment, or a reboot. Oftentimes we hold onto relationships that God has clearly told us to take a break from or to close the door on the relationship all together. We rid ourselves of and disconnect from some relationships that we should not, and we keep others that are glaringly toxic. Why is that? We should want to know the difference and make better choices.

Questions I often ask: How can we know the difference between the ones that we should keep and the ones that we should let go of? When people find themselves sacrificing their peace on a day-to-day basis that should be a big indication in my opinion that people should look into making a change or even consider moving on. Know when to let go. One of the things I have learned about people is that you become like the people you surround yourself with. If you surround yourself with people who are toxic, you eventually will become toxic.

It is important to reevaluate occasionally: Who is in my circle? Never cease to pray and ask God for the purpose of the people surrounding you. Ask more questions: How have I been a light or set an example in the circle of influence? Am I having a positive influence over them or are they having a negative influence over me? Take some time to reflect on the relationships you currently have, the ones who are most important and closest to you. Again, ask yourself questions first before you look at the areas where you feel the "crazy" has shown up. Maybe you are not like me and don't allow your emotions to get the best of you . Perhaps you feel this is too much. However, I can almost guarantee we all need to reboot our relationships. Family, business, marriage, ministry, friendships, there will come a time at some point in our lives where we need to make sure we are being all we need to be as it pertains to our relationships.

ꕥ

Dear Heavenly Father,

This one is a tough one for me, but I believe that you give, and you take away and seasons come and go. This is my season to be okay with rebooting my relationships and to reevaluate what purposes they serve. I need you to lead and guide me every step of the way.

In Jesus' name, Amen

ꕥ

"And he changeth the times and the seasons: he removeth kings, and setteth up kings: he giveth wisdom unto the wise, and knowledge to them that know understanding." (Daniel 2:21 KJV)

Reboot Your Communication

Effective communication is something that we never stop learning, growing, and revisiting how to move forward. Communication in relationships, if it is healthy, helps those involved learn how to love each other more and more. I often take the time to remind myself what it says in Proverbs, *"...with all thy wisdom get an understanding"*

This is one scripture of wisdom that will follow me wherever I go. I have been pressured to feel guilty with many friends and family because people feel I don't take up for them. This is not the case at all, it's just that I try my best to understand where people are coming from and keep it right there with them. Communication is so crucial and understanding each other's style can help avoid misunderstandings. People have their own way of communicating and need to know they are being heard regardless of their communication style. I think Dr.

Gary Smalley provided a great case for this in his best-selling book, *The Five Love Languages!* This book pertains to marriages; however, I happen to see where it can apply to all relationships in your life.

We all come from different backgrounds, we all learn at a different pace, and we don't all express our love the same way, so if we keep these elements in mind, we will be surprised how our responses to people will result in better outcomes.

Empathy is seeing the situation from the other person's perspective. You must have the ability to empathize with others you are in relationship with. Love being the ultimate trump card will always win. Finally, let the Golden Rule govern all your relationships so that you can be better and be more fulfilled. What you filter in is what will come out. Whatever comes out is the flavor people will taste. What type of lasting impression would you like to leave in your relationships? As a Christian, I believe we should exemplify love and empathy, which are both characteristics of the true love of Jesus Christ. We should not leave a bad taste in people's mouths. We should leave an impression that will leave people wanting to befriend us and wanting to come back for more conversation and great fellowship, time and again.

ꕥ

Dear Heavenly Father,

I don't always communicate the best way I should. I don't always understand the best way to communicate. I am asking you to help me in the way I speak to every person in my life. Help me to give a Godly response that pleases you.

In Jesus' name, Amen

ꕥ

"Do not let any unwholesome talk come out of your mouths, but only what is helpful for building others up according to their needs, that it may benefit those who listen." (Ephesians 4:29 NIV)

Reflections from my daughter Danielle J. Bonds

Finding Value in Yourself First

One of my favorite things to discuss with anyone who is willing to listen is the importance of finding value in yourself before being open to any type of relationship as an adult. It took me a while to grasp this concept throughout my childhood and teen years, as it probably does for most people. One thing my mom, Neesha, taught me was that it was okay to let go of those one-sided relationships and really take the time to learn the lesson in why that person entered my life for that season. Doing this made me examine myself and remember what value I brought to the relationship.

Romantic relationships are not the only relationships that we settle in. Sometimes it is the relationships with friends or even family members that we settle in just because of how long we have known them. Just because they are family, or a long-term friend does not mean you have to give up pieces of yourself to maintain the relationship. Sometimes you might need to step away for a season to regain your mental and emotional energy. Stepping away might be challenging, but there is purpose in it if you also allow God to be with you during that season. I took four steps to find value in myself before being open to any new relationships, and yes, that included my relationship with my husband.

Step 1. I consulted with God about it. I was honest about what I wanted in my relationships with my family, and my friends, and what I wanted in my husband. How open are you really with God about the things you want? Are you not praying for certain things because you feel they are too small or out of reach? God cares about the concerns of our hearts. Just talk to him and allow him to comfort you. Pray about it, and as my Auntie Shanna would say, "put it on the shelf," meaning that you will allow God to deal with it after you release it. In that place was where God was able to remind me of my value.

Step 2. I decided to walk away when a relationship no longer honored my value. I made up my mind that though I might be uncomfortable for a time, the sacrifice would be worth it. There will be a period of sadness, overthinking, memories, and feelings of loneliness because you might be mourning the time spent or that specific period.

Step 3. I sought wise counsel and therapy. In situations like this, you cannot gather advice from everyone. Only get advice from people who have been through similar situations. Even the most healed version of you needs wise counsel. It's about the maintenance of the soul. There are so many beliefs that need to be debunked.

Step 4. Forgive those who have hurt you. Did you know that forgiveness is more about you than the other person? You don't have to wait for someone to apologize or understand to remove the hurt from your soul. Healing is the priority and leaving a dirty wound open will cause an infection. And if you are having a hard time doing this, see Step 1.

Chapter Ten

Grace Grace Grace

This is one of those areas that I think, in every relationship, if you are a human being, it can consume every part of your soul. Okay! Maybe it's just my soul—as I think of the countless times I have had challenges with others' struggles. Addictions, offenses, bad habits, rejection, abandonment, need I say more?

One might say: Why is it any of your business? What is it to you? You need to let people grow. You need to just accept people as they are. Easier said than done. You can't do that when you were created to love people. You cannot leave them in their issues if you know you have the answers to help them navigate their situation. Even though we personally don't have the answers, but through each of us, God supplies what each other needs, and that includes presenting relationships that can cause healing to our souls.

First, we all have some form of a struggle in life, which can knock us off our feet. We all have a time or a place where we will hopefully heal and release our baggage. The biggest part of this factor is that it does affect those around you. It can be family, friend, or foe. It can affect work or play. Thinking back over the years of relationships that are close to me, I held them probably too close. I recall a season in my life where I became so angry with a friend who was like a little sister to me. I mean, come on, I would say to myself, you know who you are, you know how to pass this test! I became angry when it appeared her lifestyle did not match up or line up with who I knew God called her to be. Why did that matter so much to me? Didn't I have enough to be worried about?

It's one of those things, when you care about people so much, that you want to keep them on the straight and narrow. You want to be their personal guardian. Have you ever wanted everyone to kind of have kindred spirits? It cuts down on the struggle of your trial. Right? Wrong! Well, I did not know this in my younger years. I had to mature to understand this and allow God to teach me where I was missing it in this aspect in my relationships. As disappointing as the decisions that my friend made were, they should not have affected my days, or feeling as if they had a reflection on me.

I personally think my biggest letdown in life has been watching friends close to me change for the worst. I wanted all my friends to stay the same wonderful "Christian" I knew when I met them. Well, how well did that work out for me? Horribly. When people changed, I tended to avoid them because of their struggles. I would abandon my friend. I was tired of watching them struggle, so I backed away. Isn't that funny how I wanted to be all in when I thought I had control over their situation, but I wanted to be all out when I discovered I did not have control. I left the scene of being a part of their life, not once but several times. Thank God I matured, and friendships were restored. Could we then speak of the struggles? Yes, and it was for our mutual growth and our learning.

Now don't get me wrong, if someone's struggle is affecting you to the point where you join in and it changes your standards, then a shift that protects you physically, mentally, spiritually and emotionally may need to happen in the relationship. You must take care of you first before you can help anyone else. It doesn't mean it always has to end the relationship tragically or with major opposition. Honesty about where you are individually is always best. And realizing that just because you are bothered by someone else's struggle, it does not give you permission to interfere with their life. Interference, throwing digs, silent treatment, abandonment, all the above were relationship lessons learned!

Remember to always:

- Allow God to be God in people's lives
- Let them off the hook; we all disappoint someone from time to time.
- Learn to pray and not prey.
- Understand it's them today, but it maybe you tomorrow. How would you want to be treated?

Grace Breaks the Cycle

My relationship with my family has been challenging throughout the years, and I never really understood why. Why am I so sensitive to the way we communicate? Why do I jump on the defensive and then become offended by them? I have often struggled in this area; one of the most important relationships in my life is the one with my family. Let me stop right here and just state, my family is amazing. They are resilient, anointed, smart, caring, loving, giving, discerning, prophetic, and the list goes on. So, what's the problem? I realize it's me, but why do things drive me crazy when it comes to family relationships? Why am I so sensitive? Why do I wear my feelings on my sleeve?

Why do I respond to certain things in life the way I do? I get my feelings hurt because I just want my family to acknowledge me and acknowledge my feelings. I am still learning to be prefect this area.

I have had some insight on the why. The enemy, "the devil," knows that relationships are so important to me. I know my family loves me and I love them; the struggle comes when we don't agree. Offense raises its ugly head. We can either offer grace, or we can choose to live on the offensive. I say this often, "I forgive. I'm not mad," but I have chosen to put up walls to make sure I protect certain areas of my life. I recognize that in most cases people are not trying to cause offense. Most people want peace and want you to see the love they have to offer. I highly recommend the book by John Bevere, *The Bait of Satan*.

When we are emotionally immature, no matter how spiritual we are, the maturity we lack will eventually breed offense. When what you are hearing is off, your emotions are reacting to your interpretation of what you think you hear or what you think the other person meant for you to hear. If we become aware of different communication styles this will help lessen misunderstandings in our relationships.

All of us encounter it at some point in any authentic relationship. We experience that awful moment when what you said or how you acted was totally misinterpreted. Is it always necessary to address the situation quickly so as not to allow the offense or misunderstanding to fester? When is the offense too small to address? When is the offense too big to overcome? We all must ask ourselves these questions. Relationships should grow and not be filled with a life of painful offenses and toleration. God intended for us to fellowship and enjoy one another. Let's decree health in every area of our life, spiritually, emotionally, physically, and relationally. Extend grace to each other the next time offense tries to rise up. Pray for healing and restoration in every area.

What area do you need to extend grace?

____

____

____

____

____

ꕤ

Dear Heavenly Father,

I pray for the heart of grace to continue to rest with me my entire life. Your grace and mercy carry me daily, I don't know where I would be. I ask for forgiveness in the areas I have failed to extend grace in my relationships. I am reminded of the grace you extend to me daily. I desire to heal from hurts and offenses, and most importantly to forgive. I receive the grace to grow in this area.

In Jesus' name, Amen

ꕤ

"As it is written: 'He has scattered abroad His gifts to the poor; His righteousness endures forever.' Now he who supplies seed to the sower and bread for food will supply and multiply your store of seed and will increase the harvest of your righteousness. You will be enriched in every way to be generous on every occasion, so that through us your giving will produce thanksgiving to God ..." (2 Corinthian 9:8-11 MSG)

Reflections by my sister Tiffany Crawford

Grace is not easy to extend, especially when you have been hurt, but it is a requirement for any fruitful relationship. My daily prayer: Lord, grant me grace so that I can extend it to the loved ones in my life. That sums it up.

"Let your conversation be always full of grace, seasoned with salt, so that you may know how to answer everyone." (Colossians 4:6 NIV)

Chapter Eleven

The Great Escape

When I was a little girl, my sister, Shanna, and I would go into our closet and take empty milk crates, stack them together side by side, and place the prettiest pillowcases on top of them and make us a little table inside of our closet. We grabbed as many unused blankets and pillows as we could to make us the greatest homemade sofa to sit on. We sectioned off the closet to create this space to look different than our outside world. We had books and journals and flowers on the little table. It was our escape to have peace. This was our getaway from the junky bedroom, away from the noise of hearing the different family dynamics that would go on inside our home. We hid away from the other children, the frustrations, the busyness of life going on outside those closet doors. We found an escape inside a giant closet large enough to be a small bedroom. As I am typing this, I am thinking of how small that closet is now. In our minds it was a safe place to de-stress and to declutter our minds. This was our place to have peace and quiet. Even as children, we learned to take what we had access to and create something else. Calgon takes us away.

Today as an adult, I still have those moments where I feel like I have to find that place of peace and quiet, and if I don't run away to that safe place, I won't have any time to think or have peace.

I believe everyone needs a time of reprieve and a time to relax their minds. No matter how great you have it in any of your relationships, I honestly believe there is a time for our "Great Escape." This type of escape is good, a time to break away from the noise to write, or to breathe and relax from the regular scheduled program. It is time to listen to God and hear what the next assignment is going to be. I'm guilty as charged for not always taking the time to escape when I know I should. We all have a need for quiet time every day in our relationship with God; it is so needed in order to regroup and hear. I also am aware that it is in these times of escape I become a nicer person to myself and to others.

Boundaries

It never ceases to amaze me how this word is such a powerful word and yet can be so offensive when it comes to setting the meaning in place. Crossing the line in relationships has no respect of persons. We all have done it at some time or another. We all have to set boundaries, respect boundaries, learn how to understand, and then realize we, along with other people, will sometimes overstep boundaries. The determination it takes to respect boundaries and put them into practice is harder for some than others.

My own personal experience has been that I usually don't have boundaries when it comes to those I love. I usually allow freedom to reign. Getting married so young and growing up in a big family did not really allow me the gift of setting boundaries.

I allowed all my siblings to have free range to my bedroom, raid my refrigerator at any time, enjoy coming over all the time, and so on and so forth. I had children young, so the same kind of went with them also. Usually, you won't get offended by people setting boundaries unless you happen to have crossed them and the response happens to be a negative experience.

The "Just In Case" Escape

The unavoidable part of life is pain in one area or another. I have experienced loss and grief of loved one's multiple times. I remember being a young teenager about thirteen or fourteen, and our youth pastor, Minister House, became sick with cancer. She became a very good friend of my mom when they joined my childhood church. She was our musician and was over the youth choir. Sis House brought a beacon of hope and love and charisma to our church. It did not hurt that her daughters were the same age as my sister Shanna and myself, so we had instant friends. Finally, we had landed in a safe place of friendship and had a home away from home. When Minister House got the news of cancer, I can remember the youth being asked to pray and fast for her healing.

I remember for the first time fasting three days and three nights. I remember wanting God to answer my prayer. Well, she passed away and my friends were left here without a mom. I did not understand this at all. It was my very first experience of feeling the hurt of grief. I share this story with you as a reference, that when you try to escape things in life from an unhealthy place, it usually stems from a place of trauma or experience.

From that moment on I had a just-in-case escape plan in my mind. It truly is the opposite of faith because it is fear that is more present than faith. I am speaking to the emotional escape that comes so you can try to figure things out "just in case" the plan does not exactly work the way you desire.

Life is full of surprises, and you won't be able to escape unless you decide to lie down and die. Is this an option? Of course not. I have had to look at other options of how to cope with hurt rather than escape.

It's no secret that people walk around daily frustrated with the journey called life and will avoid and hide from the pain. I am guilty as charged. One of the greatest ways to do this is to cut people off if they have caused us pain. Escaping is one of the ways people cope in life. When they have seen behavioral patterns that scare them or have hurt them, it will cause most to back away. That familiar feeling of hurt will cause many to begin shutting down emotionally or sometimes shutting people out altogether.

Avoidance is a form of escaping, and it is not healthy, because one way or another you will have to face the giant called grief and adversity in the face. Loss and grief will come in all shapes, forms, and fashions when dealing with human beings. Man was not meant to be here on earth always, so therefore we must learn how to embrace all journeys of life and avoid trying to escape the feelings we have about grief and loss. Lean into the feelings you have and seek counsel to help you to live and manage when there is a loss. Lean on God for guidance and direction on how to manage after the disappointment comes in your life, especially unexpected loss through death.

Escaping Shame

Shame keeps you away! If you think the broken or painful relationships in your life stay away because of arrogance and pride, anger and unforgiveness, you may be right, but all these eventually lead to shame. It is the enemy's job to keep us in hiding and isolation, hidden from our relationships. Are you hiding?

I have learned in my own relationships that people don't just stay away to avoid you or to hurt you.

I truly believe once healing takes place shame has to flee. To be transparent, when I am not feeling my best self, I tend to shut down, hide, not make any phone calls, not really want to make any visits or connect with people. I want to feel my best self, not necessarily that I have done anything so sinfully wrong, I just know that when I am not feeling my best self it causes me to hide. During my teenage years, there were a lot of missing pieces in my family dynamics. My mom and dad struggled tremendously in their marriage. Not knowing all the details of what went on in their relationship, I do recall after a while my dad began to stay away. As I got older, I realized that I was one of those people who brought my father to shame, for the disappointments that I felt he brought upon the family. That was not my place, nor was it respectful to always remind him when he came around of the things that I felt he was not doing for me and my siblings. I was told by my husband many times that I was very disrespectful and needed to put a check on myself about the conversations I would have with my dad and the way I spoke to him. It took me a while to realize that I was angry and wanted to cause him shame in hope he would change his ways and come back to our family.

I do believe that I do not have enough power to bring any change. One of the major lessons is prayer changes things people do not. Loving kindness will draw people, shame will push them away and make them escape the painful areas of their life. This is probably one of the largest areas in my life that I had to forgive.

I recall being at a family reunion when the Lord spoke to me and said this is the year for you to forgive your dad. I went over to him after an hour and told him I apologized for all the things I held against him.

I was ready to release him to the Father and respect him for what he had to offer me as my father. What a heavy burden was released. I escaped from holding judgment anymore. I believe that I became free, and I freed my father from shame, that is, in relation to me and him. We have a great relationship now. I know there are still things he prefers not to talk about, but every now and then he speaks to the things which he could have done differently in relation to my mom as well as me and my siblings.

You cannot go back and undo the past, but what you can do is ask God to help you to heal and move forward to the future. I am reminded of the scripture and a quote: *"...forgetting those things which are behind us and pressing toward the mark of the prize of the high calling of God which is in Christ Jesus."* (Philippians 3:14 KJV)

I would miss the high calling of God and the prize if I held onto the past and didn't move away from the shame. So, I continue to do inventory of my heart to make sure forgiveness is always present.

I encourage you to take the time to have a great escape for yourself. Take time to relax and unwind and rejuvenate your heart and soul. Make sure it's for your own health and not escaping due to unforgiveness.

I am convinced now more than ever that those who want to help people and judge and imprison them because of painful experiences, then they are the ones that will carry the pain, the ones who will not escape.

Escaping Fear

Learning how to escape fear, I can honestly say throughout my entire life I have embraced a just-in-case attitude. Even knowing very well that I cannot control the future, that my life is in God's hands and not in my own, I have still wrestled with fear. Fear of my future; fear in parenting in raising fear of my children's future; fear of death, fear of divorce, fear of not being valued. Living your life in fear will handicap you from faith to believe God has your life and a good future in His hands. Recognize where fear exists and renounce it immediately. One of my favorite scriptures I must quote often when fear raises its ugly head is found in God's word.

"Casting down imaginations, and every high thing that exalted itself against the knowledge of God, and bringing into captivity every thought to the obedience of Christ ... " (2 Corinthians 10:5 KJV)

I now refuse to allow the spirit of fear to overtake me and tear me down. I live a life of faith and trust that God's plans for me are never to harm me. As long as He lives within me, I can get through anything. So, fear has been and will continue to be conquered in Jesus' name.

Choosing to get rid of the shame that comes from fear and accepting God's healing is the sure way to freedom. Freedom allows our growth and personal development to mature. When we choose to remain with shame, we are not trusting God to lead and guide us, and we act as if we don't know that He will take care of us and that His will is what's best for us.

Escape to Joy

Now let me start off by saying that one of the things that is closest to my heart is to have joy! It is my heart's desire to see people happy and to have an escape from the joy that will give you strength. I didn't realize that there is a difference between happiness and joy. But there is. Happiness can come and go. One day you're happy, one day you're sad. One day you're up, one day you're down. But the difference between having joy and unspeakable joy during stress, trauma, frustration, testing, and trials, is that even during everything you're going through, you will not allow anything to steal your joy. This does not mean you will not cry; this does not mean you will not feel the effects of painful experiences in your life, this just means that you are trusting the God of all creation and trusting his word that the joy of the Lord will be your strength. The joy that only comes from on high. My escape to joy usually means getting on a plane and traveling to a serene Caribbean Island where I can lie on beautiful white beaches and swim in the crystal blue sea, where I can look at the land and see the sand surrounding my feet. Where I can go to a place where there is no cell phone accessibility. I welcome the low accessibility to Wi-Fi and get some needed rest because the normal demands of my life cease for a moment.

I escape to my place of joy and peace. Every vacation comes to an end, and it is back to the regular scheduled program. However, our regular schedule should be filled with joy whether we are on a vacation or not. How do we create a space where we can escape to joy in our minds, our hearts, and in our day-to-day living? We must yield to a total dependency upon the rock that is higher than us, the solid rock that is Jesus. It may sound like a cliché, it may sound like it's impossible, but I must tell you personally that this relationship is one of the most important relationships you will have in your life. There is a joy that you can experience that the world cannot take from you.

There have been times when I have had very tragic things happen within my family members, and to watch them still be able to laugh and function means that they had to escape to a place where the supernatural joy would overshadow them. I must include myself in this. There is no other joy than knowing that God has your back. That you can escape from your present circumstances to the safest place in the whole world. The place where you feel love, joy, and peace. Yes, we have talked about many areas of the escape, but I believe that this is by far the greatest escape that you need to embrace for your life, when you choose to escape to Joy.

There is another form of "the great escape" which is not the healthiest. I will start by sharing a personal story. For years, the most wonderful time of the year for my family was Christmas. We had many trials in our family, but I would always focus on the good times. I can remember vividly the trials, but I can speak to the joys of our good times which outweigh the struggles.

One Christmas, I made the mistake of changing the name of our annual family Christmas Eve gathering. I was offended by one of my siblings for making a comment about the title of our invitation. Not really finding it necessary to go into detail, I want to share about how my offense turned into a choice of "I am never hosting our annual family Christmas event anymore! I will start my own tradition with, figuratively speaking, 'my four and no more.'" To be honest, that was not going to work for me too long because of the way God created my DNA and the joy of having all my gigantic family around. I decided to allow one statement to cause me to be so sensitive that I was going to escape the pain of offense and just quit an event that brought so much joy to everyone including myself.

Have you heard the phrase: fool me once shame on you, fool me twice shame on me? Well, I can recall times over the years where I would wear this statement and try to practice it like a ritual. I immediately would take on the attitude: I don't have to do this anymore, realizing I would not allow anyone ever to have a chance to take advantage of me! "You will not take my meekness for weakness" was just one of the many phrases I used to protect myself.

So, I began to escape the relationship. As a matter of fact, if any person or experience ever began to look like something in the past that represented any kind of hurt or pain, I would "avoid it like a plague." This is one of the quickest ways to escape the great emotion called hurt. Making sure you don't stick around for another opportunity to be wounded or hurt is dangerous because it means you miss out on the healing when it comes as well. The famous phrase "hurting people hurt people" is so true.

My truth remains. No matter what, I have come to understand that most of the time people don't set out to cause you pain, especially those who love you, but the ugly can come out and we can be super sensitive which will allow us to not only become offended but escape a very great relationship. My intentions are to stay determined to be open minded to believing the best about people, and trust God that I am doing the right thing by remaining open. Refusing to escape, unless the relationship becomes toxic. God knows, and He shows. Time will heal and time will tell. Stay flexible and allow your heart to remain flexible.

Lessons Learned:

- Going through trials and tribulations in life, you will find out what you are made of.
- Get under the situation and be calm.
- A soft answer turns away wrath.
- Avoid grievous words; they stir up anger.
- It's okay to escape if your heart is clean
- A heart like yours, God that's what I want.

ꙮ

Dear Heavenly Father,

I know that in my life I should let you help me to escape to you and you are alone. Casting my cares upon you because you care for me. Help me to develop a new level of trust to know that you can heal all my broken heart. You are Jehovah Rapha, my healer, and my desire is to look to you and escape to your presence today and always

In Jesus' name, Amen

ꙮ

"There hath no temptation taken you, but such as is common to man: but God is faithful, who will not suffer you to be tempted above that ye are able; but will with the temptation also make a way to escape, that ye may be able to bear it." (1 Corinthians 10:13 KJV)

Reflections from my daughter Kristen M. Dean

The most important relationship you will ever have is the one with God, but that's another conversation. The second most important conversation is the one you have with yourself. This relationship will set the tone for every other relationship you have in your life. We underestimate and overuse the term, "love yourself." Have you ever taken the time to think about what that means?

Have you ever been in love, like deeply in love with another person? I'm talking about the type of love where you want to spend all your time with them, you took the time to get to know them patiently, and even forgave quickly. You liked and even accepted everything about them. Yet, oddly enough, we don't think enough of ourselves to give the same love. We often depend on the person we are loving to be enough. We want to put the responsibility on others to love someone we have treated so poorly.

I discovered at thirty-two years old that I was never properly loving me. I didn't value me or what I wanted. I didn't take the time to discover what I truly liked or what the best attributes were about me. Although I walked around confidently, I didn't think I deserved more than the bare minimum. In turn, every relationship in my life became a personal project to do everything I could to be the most perfect and easiest person to love. I was so unaware of this that I would profess things I believed were true.

I professed things like "This is just how I am" or "My feelings don't get hurt." I built up a hard shell because I never thought that what I felt was more important than the feelings of those around me. I never thought that the things that concerned me superseded what everyone else was feeling.

People labeled me strong, confident, honest, direct, and I gave off this unbreakable vibe. It wasn't until I was sitting in a counseling session with my husband that my lack of acknowledgment for how I truly felt about me was revealed. Everything stemmed from the thought of being unworthy. I'm not sure where that came from, but immediately I wanted to right this wrong. Slowly my eyes began to open. I began to see me. I became in tune with what I wanted and felt as opposed to what was expected of me. The biggest freedom began when I surrendered my feelings to God and was reminded that I am a daughter of the king of the universe, and he loves me! He cares about my insignificant thoughts and feelings! My mind was blown!

God loving me gave me permission to take a second to think about what my wants and desires were. I took the time to uncover my dreams, and I broke free of the settlement spirit that had attached itself to me. Wouldn't you know that it led to me loving others better? It led to me truly breaking free of the molds that I was trapped in from a very young age. As I get to know and love who God has truly made me to be ... the possibilities are endless.

Don't get me wrong! It takes some adjusting for those who you have been in relationship with for years. Some will even try to hold you to what you've "already shown them." Break free and love yourself anyway. Surrender the idea that you are shrinking or holding back and loving yourself will be something you can sustain! You can't! Eventually ... the you God made will come out.

To conclude, do you know you enough to love you? Or are you busy getting to know other people and shapeshifting to the you that they need? Raise the standard of your other relationships by getting the relationship with yourself in check. People will only love you as well as you love you.

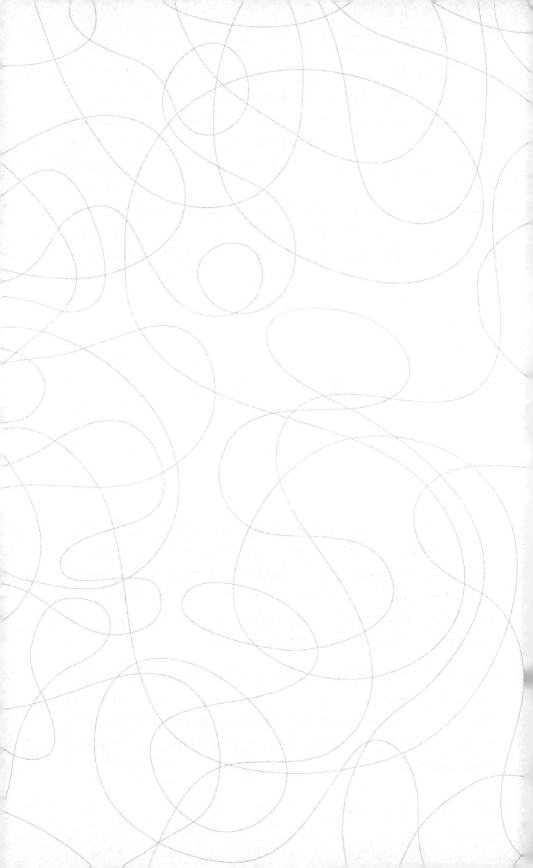

Chapter Twelve

Emotions

Emotion is defined as a natural instinctive state of mind deriving from one's circumstances, mood, or relationships with others. It is also considered an instinctive or intuitive feeling as distinguished from reasoning or knowledge. Let me be very clear when I say we were created to have and embody emotions. God gave us emotions for a reason. They were given to us as a gift to be used by us, not for us to be used.

We need people and people come with emotions. We cannot live alone, and that means we can't live apart from the emotions that come with the people we are in relationship with. We are not created as an island, and it takes people to make life work. We thank God for the world, the places we can travel, other countries, states, cities, jobs, homes schools, churches, and all the places in which people are able to experience relationships.

I believe we were designed to give Him glory throughout our life, and to fulfill what His purpose is for us on the earth. I also know for sure, God designed relationships and for us to experience love through life and people. It was His idea. Sometimes relationships can be so beautiful and sometimes we experience the ugly with people. It can feel like its unbearable. Hence the title of the book. But let me remind you, it's worth it to be in relationship with God's creation in humanity. Don't forsake the good because of the bad you may experience.

The Bible mentions in Psalm 23 that we all walk through a dark valley at times, but God never leaves us. And it says we walk through, meaning there is always an end to even our darkest of days, including those dark days we experience in our relationships. Consider the many, many days before the many, many days to come that make our life meaningful and full, if we allow. Crazy relationships drive us crazy because of the dynamics of human nature.

My relationship with God is so important to me, but there did come a time where I felt I needed to forgive my relationship with God. Yes, even forgive God for my disappointments. I did a lot of blaming and sometimes my finger pointed to the God who loved me and made me for love. I asked for forgiveness, and it has been part of my God-given purpose to help others find their own path to healing in relationships.

The seasons came with much hurt, where I experienced more heartache than I care to mention. I felt God had forsaken me. I felt as though maybe I had forsaken Him, and I had done something truly wrong in my life. I began to experience the word "loss" on a level I never knew before. Loss on any level can have us looking for love in all the wrong places, and often those places don't involve God. We will only find the peace and healing we need when we turn to the God who created us and created us for relationships. He gave us a manual called his Bible.

Grief, the sorrow, the pain, the past coming back to haunt me on many occasions, would keep me from turning the pages of my precious Bible. Yes, I knew truly that God hadn't turned His back on me, but if we don't stay in the truth of God's word, the world, our will, and emotions can.

Emotions tend to misguide our thinking. I can recall experiencing six deaths of friends and my stillborn grandson, in one year. I did not understand how this could be. Yes, I know the scriptures, "*... to live is Christ to die is gain ...*" I know the scripture that says these words are meant to bring comfort, but it was difficult in the moment.

God never sins and never wrongs you or I in these dark moments. However, I can think of countless situations where we have put God in prison. We don't want to speak to Him or give God the chance to speak to us, upset because we think He is not there. He has not been there for us the way we thought that He should be there. Maybe we thought He forgot about us. He didn't answer me when I called, so just forget it! Dare I say we may have even said, "Forget Him, He was not there for this or that, then I'll just say, forget God."

So many believers today are only a result or circumstance away from having those same thoughts. Some unbelievers already feel this way as a direct result of their pain from a tragedy that happened in life that took them to a downward turn. It brought about so much pain and torment that they disconnected from our creator. Emotions are dangerous ammunition in a weapon locked and loaded directly at our purpose in relationships and connection with God's family. Put on the full armor of God found in Ephesians 6:10-18. Reflect, restore, and renew a right-thinking attitude toward the women and men of God you were created to be in relationship with. Remember it is worth it, and the God who is more than enough wants you to experience all the joys that come from healthy and sometimes crazy relationships. Emotions can get the best of you in your relationships.

Reflection from my sister Deborah Anthony

Our God created us with relationships in mind. He did not want to just look at all he created and say, "Wow this is just great." He created man and woman to have a relationship from the foundation of the earth. So, the relationship was on purpose and, well, what comes with it is a series of emotions that essentially lead us through life and the rise and fall of how we treat others and how we treat ourselves. It seems that when we find ourselves very challenged, and we feel our emotions are out of control, there is a sense of needing to regain or center ourselves with a clear position we need to take. It's funny how emotions can sometimes feel like your defense system, but truthfully, they can misguide at times. The importance of having God center relationships that are submitted and committed to him because of the rollercoaster can be real.

We must understand the clear difference between emotions, which are a sensation in the body, and feelings, which are influenced by our thoughts. They are similar, but stem from two different places. Both can send you off your equilibrium.

I have found in my own life that emotional maturity and emotional intelligence come with time and in many cases through failed relationships. I can remember a season when I acted immature in my relationships with people because, as they say, I was in my feelings or emotions. Mismanaging people comes from values that are either non-existent or undeveloped. When I find myself fumbling over the same relationship issues time after time, I come to a complete stop and ask what part I played.

The first step to overcoming the highs and lows of your emotion is to stop and look in the mirror and ask yourself: What role did I play?

The second step is to get accountability and feedback from someone who loves you enough to speak the truth.

The third step is to do the work it takes to grow in emotional intelligence. It's not something that just happens. It's something that takes hard work and commitment.

Emotional intelligence is the capacity to be aware of, control, and express one's emotions, and to handle interpersonal relationships judiciously and empathetically.

As you read *My Relationships Are Driving Me Crazy*. I hope that it settles you and normalizes those emotions are a part of life but there is helping to get them under control.

ജ്ഞ

Dear Heavenly Father,

My emotions are out of control sometimes, I acknowledge that I sometimes I take things out on other people. Please forgive me Jesus. I pray for an ear to hear the gentle nudge of the Holy Spirit to speak to me and remind me of how to speak, when to speak, and how to respond in love. I pray you help me control my emotions in Jesus name.

ജ്ഞ

"He that is slow to anger is better than the mighty; and he that ruleth his spirit than he that taketh a city." (Proverbs 16:3 2KJV)

"He that is slow to anger is better than the mighty; and he that ruleth his spirit than he that taketh a city." (Proverbs 16:32 KJV)

Family Emotions

"Unless the Lord builds the house, they labor in vain who build it." (Psalm 127:1 NASB)

Part of the chorus to the song "Reflections" by Diana Ross is ringing through my head right now: Reflections of the way life used to be...

The memories I once knew are not a vague dream. One thing I will never forget is the moment when I began to cherish my family. I mean early on being the oldest of eight children caused me to have a spirit of shame. I recall being parked outside the thrift store as my mom left me and my siblings in the car while she went in to try to find uniform shirts second hand so she could have enough money to continue our education in private Christian school. Or when she would search for coats to keep us warm from the zero and below cold Chicago winters. I was only thinking of myself as pedestrians would walk past our station wagon and begin to count all the little heads they saw sitting in the car. "So many," they would say. I also remember road trips and mini vacations with our family where my dad and mom wanted us to have some fun. I would ride in the car the entire two to three hours to Wisconsin with my head down so people would not see all the entourage of kids. Looking back and thinking, was this all a dream? No, it was very real and stemmed from very real feelings. Now I know something that I did not know then, it is very important to cherish your family.

Fast-forward to my current situation today, and you will find that I cherish my family. Our blended family, finding out I have two other sisters outside of my parents, came to rock my entire world. Our family dynamics needed them in our lives, so I am forever grateful. I would not want to do life without them. Family dynamics can be so much fun and so much work all at the same time. No matter what stage we are in, we need our family, and we need each other.

Parenting Emotions

Being a parent was something I never really thought about as a child. I was pregnant with my first child at eighteen and shortly, twenty months later, here comes number two. I have three daughters I gave birth to, and one bonus son blended with my husband. I am grateful for the gift of parenting. It was not always easy, but I think I mastered it well.

I think I was a great mom. I did my best to try to bring balance and structure as well as enjoyment to my children while they were toddlers and adolescents. Twenty-plus years later, I am faced with some regrets and desires where I would have done things differently. Every parent has thoughts of things they wish they could have done, or to have made different decisions. I do realize parenting is a learning and growing experience. No matter how many classes you take, or books you read, it is a trial-and-error gift. I am grateful for the relationship with my children, all four of them. Yes, we have had our challenges that I am usually transparent about, much to their annoyance; I share too much. The transparency does not go over very well. I have learned so much, and I would not trade parenting for anything in the world. I love my children and the gift they are in my life. Now that they are adults, worries and cares seem to have gone to another level. I truly thought I would have been able to see the easier "yellow brick road." Boy, was I wrong! Instead, trusting God and my prayer life went to another level.

Sometimes I have to ask, "Lord, will it ever end? I mean, really, my heart's desire was to attempt to be done with this part of life."

It was so much easier when they were small, the worries were less, you had more control over at least the driving arrangements. God, you knew exactly what I would be experiencing. The one thing that I know for sure about this season of adult parenting is that your prayer life must increase, for your stress to decrease. I mean, hopefully. I have been blessed beyond measure with three daughters biologically, and one bonus son. At this present time, I have four grandchildren. I must admit that these have been some of the hardest and most challenging times of my life. Watching the pain of your adult children walk through the journey of hurt and pain. Now don't get me wrong, there has been lots of joy, and lots of laughter and excitement. Yes, for this I am so grateful, but I cannot lie, I have always just wanted a little break. Truly that was not God's idea, to catch a break, when He made us parents.

I am grateful for the opportunity to watch them grow and learn. I acknowledge most parents feel one of two ways: Where did I go wrong? or, I did an amazing job.

Either way, it will keep you on your knees. God's plan in the life of relationships was not to control, but to release the control. If ever there is a time where Proverbs 3:5-6 needed to be branded in the brain, it is the season of adult parenting.

"Trust in the Lord with all thine heart, and lean not to thine own understanding; in all thy ways acknowledge Him and He shall direct thy paths." (Proverbs3:5,6 KJV)

- Pray with them, not just for them.
- Talk to them, not at them.
- Listen to them and wait to see if a response is requested.
- Share with them your experience and pray they can learn from them.
- Remind them of Matthew 6:33 and don't stop.

"But seek ye first the kingdom of God, and his righteousness; and all these things shall be added unto you." (Matthew 6:33 KJV)

These simple reminders can be the glue that builds strong relationships within the different family dynamics for years to come. Create memories worth remembering because you took the time to do relationships differently the way God intended.

Pastor Shirley Caesar wrote a song that really sums up how I feel with adult parenting:

"My sister's little boy came in the kitchen one evening while she was fixing supper. And he handed her a piece of paper he had been writing on. And after wiping her hands on an apron, she took it in her hands and read it.

And this is what it said:

For mowing the yard $5. And for making up my own bed this week $1. For going to the store $.50. And playing with little brother while you went shopping $.25. Taking out the trash $1. And for getting a good report card $5. And for raking the yard, $2.

Total owed $14.75.

Well, she looked at him standing there and expecting, and a thousand memories flashed through her mind.

So, she picked up a pen and turned the paper over, and this is what she wrote:

For the nine months I carried you

Holding you inside me, no charge

For the nights I sat up and doctored you

And prayed for you no, charge
For the time and tears
And the costs through the years
There is no charge
When you add it all up
The full cost of my love is no charge
For the nights filled with gray
And the worries ahead
No charge
For the advice and the knowledge
And the costs of your college
No charge
For the toys, school, and clothes
And for wiping your nose
There's no charge my son
When you add it all the real cost of my love is no charge.

After that mom finished talking to her little boy, he looked up at her with a great big o' tear in his eyes.

And he said, "Mama, I sure do love you."

And then, reaching out, he got the letter and turned it over, and he wrote in great big words

Paid in full.

When you add it all up the real cost of my love is no charge."

This song hits home more now than ever, having adult children. I have truly enjoyed being an empty-nester and must say that Wes and I are extremely, humbly proud of all our adult children.

God's grace is sufficient and has been through every season. I can look back at my relationship with my mom, and the thoughts flood my mind now as I have adult children that I really understand my mom's heartache and prayers and worries in hoping all eight of us would live for God, and then be able to take care of ourselves.

I have not really apologized to my mom, but I think it's important to go back and remember the part we all played in bringing our parents some type of heartache or pain.

I just wish I had the grace to explain how much pain it is when you see your children, the ones you carried in your womb for nine months, charge you with their own pain. I also realize it's through this pain that I must understand how our Heavenly Father feels when He watches us daily forsake Him and His word, or just do something as simple as not trusting Him. Taking matters into our own hands. My heart aches in this area. However, I must put my trust in the one who allowed me the grace to give birth to my children. I must take the time to seek the face of God on their behalf. I am not so naive to think I have arrived on my own. Someone prayed for me. My mother and father prayed for me.

It's not easy to understand all the thing's life will present with adult parenting. There will be times where all the questions will come up.

- Where did I go wrong?
- What mistakes did I make?
- Am I reaping what I have sown?

- God, will you ever bring peace?

Yes, the answer is yes! I know without a shadow of a doubt that I must learn to trust God no matter what. I must learn to run to Him on my knees. He is the provider, the healer, the restorer.

I thank God for my children. I thank God for the opportunity that God gave me to be able to have them and the time to raise them. There is a pertinent reminder however, and that is something we often forget. The word adult! They are adults and the best lesson I have had to lean into is that after they become adults they belong to God, and I have only one responsibility, which is to go to Him on their behalf. I must spend less time talking and more time praying. Less time being reactive and more time petitioning the Holy Spirit in their behalf. I thank God for the trials I have felt with adult parenting. It has taught me and is yet teaching me that I am not the savior. Jesus paid it all. I did not! I was given a job temporarily to house my children and, when they became adults, to practice the word of God!

"Love is patient, love is kind. It does not envy, it does not boast, it is not proud. It does not dishonor others, it is not self-seeking, it is not easily angered, it keeps no record of wrongs. Love does not delight in evil but rejoices with the truth. It always protects, always trusts, always hopes, always perseveres.

"Love never fails. But where there are prophecies, they will cease; where there are tongues, they will be stilled; where there is knowledge, it will pass away. For we know in part, and we prophesy in part, but when completeness comes, what is in part disappears. When I was a child, I talked like a child, I thought like a child, I reasoned like a child. When I became a man, I put the ways of childhood behind me. For now, we

see only a reflection as in a mirror; then we shall see face to face. Now I know in part; then I shall know fully, even as I am fully known.

"And now these three remain: faith, hope and love. But the greatest of these is love." (I Corinthians 13:4-13 KJV)

My crazy heart along with the hearts of other moms and dads all over the world will not really take the road of Proverbs 3:5-6 and we will let our head and hearts lead more than trusting our Heavenly Father. As the reminders come, I would love to encourage you as I have had to encourage myself, that God purposely designed our children, and He knows their future. Prayer is the only gift we can offer our children when they become adults. There are no words that work better in their ears more than the heavens opening and speaking to them. He is the only one that can offer adult children unconditional, everlasting love.

Let's allow our crazy hearts to love our children through our prayers. It's the best.

ꕥ

Dear Heavenly Father,

This prayer is always in my heart. I thank you for the gift of parenting, the gift of family. If I am pleasing you then I know things will work out. Help me to love unconditionally like you. It's my desire to have a heart like yours in every area of my relationships.

In Jesus' name, Amen

ꕥ

"Train up a child in the way he should go, and when he is old, he will not depart from it." (Proverbs 22:6 KJV)

Reflection from my youngest daughter Nia R. Robinson

One of the first relationships I remember was with my mom. From the beginning, I knew what kindness felt like. She was sweet and sympathetic to all my needs. I'm going to share three core memories that set the foundation for life lessons and my ever-evolving relationship with my mom.

1. Relationship with God. We woke up every morning at six a.m. to pray before school, or should I say we were woken up and forced against our will to come to her room to pray before school. I wouldn't change it for the world. Now, I'm finding myself doing the same thing in my own time. I'm forever grateful for that foundation she instilled in us because it taught us that our relationship with God is our first priority.

2. Relationships with Others. Out of the three of my sisters and I, I had the least interest in and talent towards hair care, which was my mom's profession. The worst part about it was that my introverted, anti-social nature dreaded speaking to anybody at the crack of dawn while assisting with hair. However, those times were my first introduction to customer service. I watched my mom go above and beyond basic kindness for her clients to make sure they were comfortable, and their needs were met. The love of Jesus was extended to everybody, and I saw how she poured value into everyone who sat in her chair. Those are lessons I take with me everywhere. Sometimes it takes going beyond my own comfort for the service of somebody else.

Relationships in Adulthood. When I first moved out of my parent's house, I understood that I needed to be 100 percent independent, and

I didn't want to rely on my parents for finances, bills, or emergencies. My relationship with my mom changed from co-dependency to learning how to be intentional with sustaining our relationship. I constantly catch myself before calling her and go down a small checklist: 1. Am I only calling because I need something? 2. Have I asked her how she's doing? 3. Have I considered what kind of mental and physical space she's in? Now that I'm out of the house as an adult and currently on my way to marriage, my priority is to make sure my mom knows she's valued outside of providing basic needs. Those efforts look different as I navigate through each stage of my own life. And in return, I need to be attentive to the fact that she's just as brand new to her own life's seasons as I am to my own. The more I become aware of that, the more compassion there is to lend.

Chapter Thirteen

Crisis Relationships / Cry-Sees (Answering the Cry)

My personal favorite of all relationships is being the rescuer. I might add it is one of the most dangerous of all relationships because the true and only rescuer is not of this world. Everyone has their own belief systems but although my own personal belief is that God is the only one who can truly save people in a crisis, it does not stop the human nature of a doer who immediately runs to the rescue.

When I see a *cry-sees,* I immediately run to it. Now the question here is: is this action from true relationship, or were you just answering the call?

Whether or not it is answering the call to prayer or the call to fix something, it's important to know if you are the one who should run to the rescue.

We may not even realize the need, and we answer what we think should happen and what the correct answer should be, but have we taken the time to think about things before we respond?

The first responders in the professional protection world are usually the ones who will take a hit first, but they must be prepared and trained in order to answer the call.

My family is a crisis-oriented family. I often say, when there is a crisis in our family, we show up locked and loaded and ready to pray, slay, and answer immediately. My family went through a very difficult crisis recently with the loss of my nephew, John Wesley Anthony, who took his life. He was eighteen years old, and I received the call and immediately went to answer. I prayed briefly when I received the news and went into crisis mode. I raced to my brother and sister's home desiring to do all I could for them and my nieces. My eyes are filled with tears as I recall this tragedy, which is still as fresh as it was less than a year ago. My family showed up locked and loaded. We answer crisis well, but is our relationship built only in crisis? I was told by a friend that it's my family culture. As much as I want to protect and get offended, I realize that some elements of this statement are true.

I share this story in hopes of reminding myself to evaluate my relationships and the foundation on which they were built. One reason is because when the crisis is over, are you still present or are you absent until the next crisis? To me this is not good. It hurts. It gives people a false sense of a relationship that may not really exist.

I can think of countless times where I heard of something that caused someone pain, and I went to comfort and console and answer the need. I am not saying just let things fall apart; however, I am saying count up the cost before you just jump out there. Are you equipped? Do you know the entire story? Does this person need you or were they just venting to you?

So many dynamics are involved in the relationship of crisis. What is a crisis, (cry-sees)?.

What do we need when you show up all the time.

People will get used to you showing up in their lives and then get terribly angry when you are not able to. Family and friends will sit back and watch you use your gift of help in troubleshooting or problem-solving and then get frustrated when you ignore and don't jump to their need. They expect you to drop everything and answer their cry for help.

Are You the Counselor or the Friend

The counselor relationship cannot be confused with friendship. When I was a little girl, I always wanted friendships. I would see others who seemed to have a lot of friends, but I felt that I was a nerdy girl, who was not popular and didn't fit in anywhere. My only friends were at church, and I considered them to be more like family.

Growing up as the oldest I had a lot of responsibilities. I realize now, I took on the role of a being a fixer and that was my way of showing how much I cared for everyone. Over time this turned me into being a person who did well at 'fixing', but on the other hand it satisfied my need for affirmation. Thus, I began the journey of being an advisor. I became known as one who could 'fix' problems, because people liked my advice and when they took it, it worked for them.

What did this do? It fed an empty void inside of me, but it also generated a situation where all my relationships developed into people who were affirming me for what I was bringing to the table. There was a question that I didn't know would inevitably come, what happens when the advisory role stops? When no one needs you, or your life faces a crisis where you can't fulfill the fixer role? What happens is that your world of relationships becomes empty.

It is at this point I found out what I was really made of. For it is at this point I was forced to examine what was really my motivation for the things I was doing and the way I was interacting with people. For when the noise stops and the busy calms down, and I no longer was fulfilling the advisor role, I had to question whether I was content with who I was. I also had to examine what relationships were left when I no longer was the one feeding the relationship with what I had to give.

I now know that quiet time was ordained by God because He wanted me to sit and listen to Him. He wanted me to embrace His Word, to be poured into and counseled by Him.

It is what I call the fueling station, something so needed in the life of a counselor. For as sure as there is breath in our bodies, we will run empty. In that state, it not only affects our mental and emotional being, it affects our physical health as well.

Opting Out

During those times when you must opt out of providing the role of being an advisor, undoubtedly your relationships suffer. The reason they suffer is because many of those relationships have thrived on what you provide for them. When you are no longer being the provider, there is hurt. The person who is used to receiving from you, now feels abandoned. They may strike out against you. It is here that you have to decide if you are going to take it personally or recognize that it is their way of expressing their pain of your seeming rejection.

The situation then also becomes one where you might be hurt to the extent that you need to forgive. When that happens, you find yourself straining with every fiber in your being that you don't want to ever go through this again. I am reminded of the saying, "get me once, shame on you; but hit me twice shame on me". Forgiveness is one of the hardest things for people to do. In any relationship when you feel as if you have been wronged, or rejected you want to nurture your wounds.

When you feel the tug of the Father saying you must forgive the person who hurt you, it's not something you want to do. You might even get angry with God. I've heard many people say that they are not going to forgive the person because they didn't do anything wrong. In God's economy, that does not relieve you of the forgiveness you must give. For when you forgive, it is as much for you as it is the other person. By letting them out of prison, you let yourself out of prison also. This is one key to living a healthy life.

How Do You Fix the Broken Relationships?

You consult the father first. You pray. Taking the time to pray and asking how to respond to a crisis is the best suggestion I can offer, especially when I am still learning to use this principle myself. God is the only one who can bring comfort and clarity in a crisis. I know God uses people, but the outcome can be so much richer if we take the time to pause, pray, and then pursue with godly wisdom before just jumping to the rescue. I am still learning, still practicing. It's a daily journey.

The Pain Reliever

As far back as I can understanding what pain was, I wanted to just make it go away, find something to remove, cover, or dissipate it. This became my ruling desire. To relieve people of their pain. "Yes, I can help." This is the beauty of the 'fixer'. You always know that you can help. Although this is a gift, it can be a real burden in our relationships. For while it may serve as a help in one sense, it can also cause major damage in another.

As an artist by profession and having a creative gift, it can be easy for me to see the problem and try to make the ugly beautiful. I have found myself minding my own business at work, or at a restaurant, or anywhere, and have overheard a conversation that caused me to leap inside with the answers. There have been so many times when there was a true dance party going on inside my head giving me the moves that could see, advise, and want to share the "fix it" to what I've heard. I'm quite sure God did not make any mistakes when he designed the "fixer", even me, but I do know He prefers us to consult Him in everything, especially when we try to fix those in our relationship community. We may be able to relate, or not, but it is imperative that we allow our minds to be still until we get marching orders to move out on before we do what think we need to do. Premature actions can cause more damage and ruin a relationship.

How many of our relationships do we try to fix? How many times does our brain immediately shift into gear when we see a situation going wrong? Our brain never stops. What we don't realize that we are standing in the way of our Daddy God by trying to help relieve people of feeling the brunt of pain life can sometimes bring.

People like me live in a place of automatic relationship repair and want to immediately go into action. My advice to you is the same as I have had to take for me, get off this train immediately! You cannot and I repeat cannot heal set free or deliver, ONLY GOD CAN!

Examine this list and see if there are signs in your life that you are trying to be a 'fixer':

- You are an immediate responder, people can count on you to respond
- You can handle lots of stress and it takes a lot for you to get burned out
- You will 99% of the time drop your own scheduled program to accommodate, enjoy or to fix a part of someone else's life
- You tend to build relationships with people who need help
- You make it a point to make things right no matter what
- You are a great troubleshooter, and people can call you and count on you to help talk them through almost any problem
- You are a person of influence
- You can change or create almost anything into something better
- You are concerned about other people and their problems more than your own
- Your desire is to see others happy and not alone
- You are very persuasive and persistent almost to the point of controlling

The best way to know when it's time to evaluate your next move is to ask these questions:

- God, what should I do, how do you want me to respond?
- Should I go?
- What do you want me to do?

The best advice ever given to me: Ask God what you should do about each situation. Unfortunately, there are times when I don't follow this advice. Promise yourself that the next time you try to fix something or someone; either through advice, or just being the wise counselor, make sure you have permission, from the person and from God. Prayer is the best way we can fix any relationship problem. We can be a bigger help on our knees, than we ever can be giving our pearls of wisdom. It may go against our nature, but it will be worth it.

List some areas you have tried to fix relationships and instead you needed to surrender by trusting the Lord.

ꕥ

Dear Heavenly Father,

Please help me to take your word and brand it upon my heart. You are the only one who can save, heal, and come to the rescue. Use me for your glory but help me to consult you first in every area of my life.

In Jesus' name, Amen

ꕥ

Reflections from my mother Dr. Alice Maria Crawford

Learning that God does not need you to solve other people's problems is a humbling revelation. Our humanity wants to be needed, to be valued, even to be esteemed. Being told that we can be more effective in prayer, than we can in person goes against everything in us. And yet, when we learn this, we have discovered a valuable key to unlocking the Kingdom of God in our lives.

God does not want to fire us from our role of helping people, rather He wants to enhance it. He wants us to understand that "without Him we can do nothing" and with Him we can do everything! Nothing is impossible. What we have to learn however, is to get in right alignment with Him. He will use our compassion, our voice, our touch – but the Words will come from Him. And they will serve as a healing balm for the one in need. They will also serve as a catalyst to propel them into the kind of action that will bring resolution to their problem.

"O taste and see that the Lord [our God] is good; How blessed [fortunate, prosperous, and favored by God] is the man who takes refuge in Him." (Psalm 34:8 AMP)

Chapter fourteen

Breaking The Cycle of Crazy

Family bloodlines have a lot to do with our inability to move forward in our lives. It also limits our ability to fight for our families, our children and our communities. One thing I am certain of is that there is an adversary that wants us to get tired and weak. It is the responsibility of the elders, to teach the next generations how to break the cycle of their past.

Generational Curses are very real to me. You may not like to use that term because it has been used very loosely in the church, with no remedy attached. It is almost a cliché', a way of excusing bad behavior. Even though we may say generational blessings are flowing more than the generational curses, we need to destroy the generational curses for they will crop again unless we do.

The only way I know to do this is to go back to the one who created us in the first place and ask Him to give you strategies on how to pray and respond. Praying for answers is a constant ritual; asking God to give me wisdom against the things that appear in my life to bring fear, doubt and unbelief. For this has been a generational curse in my family.

Every parent should want more for their children, however if we keep looking at the things that are weighing them down, by joining in the party of generational curses, then we won't ever see the Hope that is available to change. The Hope that says there is a prescription for change, we just need to tap into it and not sit back and give it power by saying, "IT IS WHAT IT IS"! It is more than breaking the cycle, it's being fully healed and moving forward to a future of healing and wholeness.

It is our responsibility, even though we may be weak in some areas, to tap into the Word of God and allow strength to rise up within us. We are not who we say we are, we are who God says we are. We can not help what happened to our parents, nor can we go back and try to fix the past, but we can allow the Word of God to fortify us to break everything in our lives that needs to be broken so we can lead the next generation forward into the plan of God. It is never too late.

We do this by setting goals, making necessary changes, establishing new traditions. My mom did this by establishing one of the best traditions we have in our family. It was speaking over our day first thing in the morning, it set the tone for the day. Even with our reluctance to do this when I was young, I found that it worked and I began to do this with my children, and now they are doing it with their children. It may not seem like a big thing, but little becomes much when you give it to God and allow the new choices, traditions, and changes to take place.

Vision Clear

By establishing a real relationship with 'vision', you will find it to be a true game changer in your life. Write the vision, and make it plain, write down everything you want to see God do in your life. Do not hold back, no matter where you are in your spiritual faith journey, no matter how much money you have, no matter, what's going on in your personal journey, SEE BIG! WRITE BIG! DREAM BIG!

It takes a clear vision to see where you are going. Vision gives us hope! Vision gives us energy to keep our eyes on our hearts desire.

"What's God going to say to my questions? I'm braced for the worst. I'll climb to the lookout tower and scan the horizon. I'll wait to see what God says, how he'll answer my complaint. And then God answered: "Write this. Write what you see. Write it out in big block letters so that it can be read on the run. This vision-message is a witness pointing to what's coming. It aches for the coming—it can hardly wait! And it doesn't lie. If it seems slow in coming, wait. It's on its way. It will come right on time." (Habakkuk 2:3 MSG)

If people can't see what God is doing, they stumble all over themselves; But when they attend to what he reveals, they are most blessed.

Glasses help give you a clearer vision than what you can see with your natural eye. I have found that it is natural tendency for people to get frustrated when things don't LOOK like what they thought it would, or when it's not happening fast enough. When this occurs, it might be the time to get some glasses. Glasses in this scenario are represent the people you go to for counsel.

There are people (glasses) who have been where you are and have conquered things you are being tested on. You don't have to rely on your own strength. We need the help of God (glasses) and others in order to regain our focus. Stay away from everyone who has blurry vision! Find those (glasses) which allow clarity and discernment.

"Escape quickly from the company of fools; they're a waste of your time, a waste of your words." (Psalm 14:7 MSG)

It is vital to your overall health that when your vision becomes so blurry that you feel that you will never SEE a way out, it is then you get some medicine for your vision. Don't give up or throw in the towel. Take the time to get with someone who can give you an eye exam and see where you problems are. A good counselor can show you how your vision got blurry in the first place? Was it from past hurts and pains, childhood experiences that you haven't forgiven?

Remember un-forgiveness will blind you! It will keep you in a place that will not allow you to move on with the vision God has given you. Un-forgiveness will blind your family, it will cause everyone to get an infection, almost like pink eye which is highly contagious. Don't try to fill your own prescription, take some time to find a person who will help assist you in your healing.

When Your Helping Becomes Your Worst Enemy

Regrettably there have been times when I experienced embarrassment from not minding my own business. There have also been those times when I have put my foot in my mouth, or I overstepped my boundaries. I confess there has been more than one time when I have identified with the biblical "Martha". Busy as a bee; buzzing around trying to help everyone and do everything myself. I was not taking the time to sit and be still and to wait on what was my next assignment. Learning how and when to be quiet and not having to offer advice or counsel is an important skill in the life of a counselor. We must take time to think, ponder, and not take the time to pause and breathe. To exhale. In our lives it is essential to have a brain dump, to allow the brain to declutter by thinking of nothing! I have had -optimistic view of life and relationships. If people show you who they are believe them!

Crazy to Rest

Rest is one of the main things you need in order to see clear! When you are tired and weighed down you will begin to blame the world, then falsely accuse, and finally become toxic to everyone you are around. The lack of rest will wear you down! You will have no patience to listen, hear, and love during times of chaos. The lack of Rest will cause a wreck in your home, job, your very life.

Rest is vital for a clear vision. When you are too tired there is no energy to go on. People, especially women, tend to give up their vision because of weariness in the mind. We are mothers, sisters, wives, daughters, teachers, creators, and usually relied upon to make everything in life work. We must make the decision that we are not all things to all men. We must rest our bodies, minds and spirits. Being all over the place causes us to make foolish decisions, become vulnerable to temptation, and most importantly it will affect our health.

This takes discipline, we have our own definition of what we need, but sometimes it's time to rewrite the prescription, what you used yesterday, may not be effective today. You may need to reposition your rest.

When God created us He knew what we could handle. It has never been our job to carry the load or handle things on our own. I am reminded of the Proverbs 31 woman, read it in the message translation if you can, she was a bad sister, so it when I read about her that I know we are capable of handling and doing things with grace, however, being as wise as she was I am sure she made the choice to rest when needed. There is rest, and it is not just sleeping, resting the mind brings necessary peace. Making choices to rest when hell is breaking lose all around you. The type of rest that may confuse people and ask, "how is she smiling"? It's because she has entered into His rest.

"Thou wilt keep him in perfect peace, whose mind is stayed on thee: because he trusteth in thee." (Isaiah 26:3 KJV)

Crazy to Choose

Life is all about choices. Making a choice to say I will not give up; I will hold on to every desire and vision that's in my heart. To do this we must first make these choices:

- Choose God!
- Choose to forgive
- Choose to heal that your children will heal
- Choose to love even in the midst of pain
- Choose to rest
- Choose to smile
- Choose to pray
- Choose to share the load
- Choose to let go of pride
- Choose to be transparent, this shows true healing
- Choose to share your testimony and help others get free
- Choose to share your vision
- Choose to fix yourself up
- Choose to look amazing and feel amazing
- Choose to encourage
- Choose to fight for your children and your family

- Choose to let go of bitterness, anger and all resentment, it breeds sickness
- Choose to stay around positive people who will not pull you down but help lift you up
- Choose to seek God first in all things for he is source of our strength
- Choose to write the vision and make it plain to yourself, your family and all who know you
- Choose victory!

"Therefore, believers, be all the more diligent to make certain about His calling and choosing you [be sure that your behavior reflects and confirms your relationship with God]; for by doing these things [actively developing these virtues], you will never stumble [in your spiritual growth and will live a life that leads others away from sin];" (2 Peter 1:10 AMP)

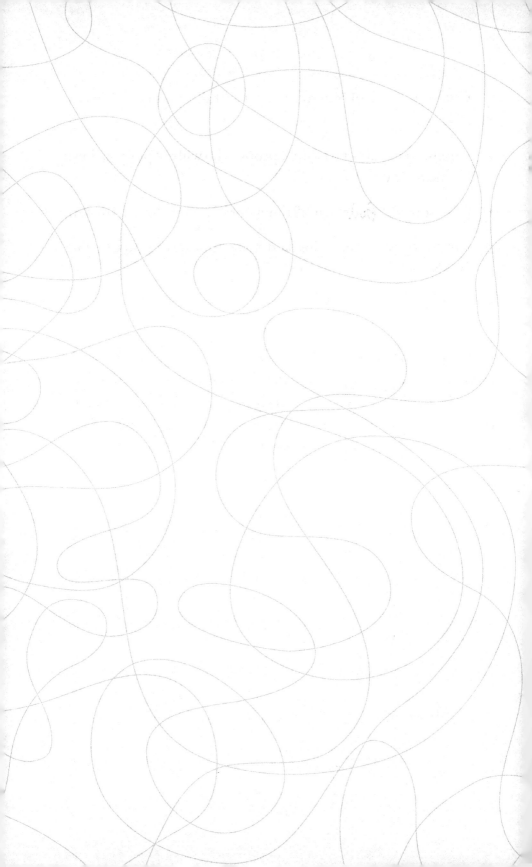

Chapter Fifteen

Restored Relationships

My heart's desire has always been to see relationships restored. I don't think there has ever been a time in my life when I decided a relationship had to be over. As you grow in life you definitely become wiser to realize some relationships are not meant to be restored. This chapter is mainly speaking to areas in life where you know without a shadow of doubt that God's intention is for restoration, sometimes even if we don't want it.

The three relationships that are the most important to me have always been:

- my relationship with God
- my relationship with myself
- my relationship with those around me; family, friends, and loved ones

The thought of a personal relationship with the Almighty Creator is a gift. Then learning how to love myself and embrace who I am is a privilege. Then the gift of being surrounded by family and friends is priceless.

Life has a way of reminding us of the relationships we take for granted. Although the love is strong and we value all three of these relationships, we can also suffer disappointment from all. We must take a deeper look inside of ourselves to avoid getting stuck in unforgiveness. I have had to learn how to find restoration in all of them. Probably one of the largest struggles that I've ever had in relationships has been in the last couple years with having to deal with loss, lack of understanding when you have put your faith and trust and hope in the God of the universe who is your daddy, and the disappointment that comes when you have trusted him like none other. Yes, forgiving God all while asking for restoration with him is probably the largest area that when accomplished will bring healing in every other single relationship.

Be *intentional* about valuing relationships. God designed relationships. They were not our idea. From the beginning of time, He said that Man should not be alone, and of course, when sin entered the world, broken relationships and brokenness were bound to happen.

Throughout the Bible there are stories of broken relationships; however, it is so funny how in the midst of the brokenness, God will use the very person that's broken to bring restoration and healing as He uses His only begotten son, Jesus Christ, to be the one to bring healing and restoration in every single relationship. I have found that as hard as it has been the last couple years, with so much pain and heartache showing up in my family, it has been nothing but God's grace that has carried me through to hold on to the relationships no matter what. I truly don't understand how people make it and restore it without having Jesus in their life, so today I would like to offer a few things which helped me with the process of healing. Every relationship has opportunity for healing.

Reflections

- Relationship with God is an unshakable confidence that God has got you and no matter what life brings, nothing can shake your relationship with the one who designed relationships and desired them from the beginning.

- Relationships with yourself would include the fruits of the spirit.

- Relationships with others would be being confident in the relationships God has put in your life.

Steps to Restoration

God has sent people for a reason into our lives, we may not actually understand the season, and it's important to understand the reason and then reconcile with yourself whether they are for a lifetime.

- Be Honest with God, yourself and each other
  "But speaking the truth in love, may grow up into him in all things, which is the head, even Christ." (Ephesians 4:15 KJV)

  "Be ye angry, and sin not: let not the sun go down upon your wrath: Neither give place to the devil." (Ephesians 4:26-27 KJV)

  "Let no corrupt communication proceed out of your mouth, but that which is good to the use of edifying, that it may minister grace unto the hearers. And grieve not the holy Spirit of God, whereby ye are sealed unto the day of redemption." (Ephesians 4:29-30 KJV)

- Take it one day at a time and embrace Daily Restoration!
  "Yet this I call to mind and therefore I have hope: Because of the Lord's great love we are not consumed, for his compassions never fail. They are new every morning; great is your faithfulness." (Lamentations 3:21-23 NIV)

- Restoring my time
  I don't know about you, but my attitude and disappointment caused a disconnect; He didn't leave me, I left Him. I asked God to renew my mind in order for me to start spending time with God and being reminded of His love for me and that He is the reason for relationships (redeem the time, make the time, forgive the time).

- Restoring my trust
  Trusting God with a nevertheless, no matter what, a true *yes* in the good and the bad, learning how to trust again (Angry, Forgiving, Trusting).

- Restoring my testimony
  Oftentimes in the storm, we forget who we are and whose we are, and misrepresent our Heavenly Father. It's important to find healing and when you have healed, you can talk about it.

- Restoring relationships with yourself

- Restore my confidence

- Forgive myself

- Speak God's word in the areas you are weak.

- Restore my want to want to

- Restore my love and passion for God, for life, for what God has called me to do

- Restore the fruits of the spirit
  The fruits of the spirit sometimes get lost in the shuffle when you are not feeling your best self. Some people fake it till they make it, and some people like me find it hard to hide the pain, and love, joy, peace, longsuffering, gentleness, meekness, faith, and temperance all shift (shifts your dry place).

- Forgive yourself

- Restored relationships with God

- Restoring my time

- Restoring my trust.
- Restoring my testimony
- Restore my Confidence
- Restore my want to want to
- Restore my love and passion
- Confidence or critical
- Restored relationships with people require giving them fully to God!

Restoration Exercise

Ask God for Healing

Write down what areas you need healing in your relationships: Where do you want to see restoration?

Believing. Write down what areas you want God to perform a miracle, the areas and the people you are trusting to God for wholeness, even the ones you have determined are completely impossible.

Encouragement. Everyone needs encouragement. Don't be selfish with the love God has given you because you have experienced brokenness.

Life is not over, and God has even more of a plan for you and your relationships, shake yourself loose and begin to encourage someone else,

Write down what areas you know you can encourage yourself and someone else.

____

____

____

____

____

Lastly, prayer. It's time to pray and prophesy over our relationships, it's time to begin to see those dry, stale areas of brokenness, to see life. Life in the midst of what looks like death.

In order to really embrace being restored, you must first acknowledge that something is broken or needs to be repaired. You also cannot blame someone else; oftentimes, we don't take ownership of our own brokenness, and when we fail to be honest about where we are, it does not allow us to heal. We need to be open with ourselves and then others, but always in love.

When all is said and done, pray without ceasing, ask God for His restoration, which is the ultimate peace in every relationship.

Take it one day at a time and embrace Daily Restoration!

"Yet this I call to mind, and therefore I have hope: Because of the Lord's great love we are not consumed, for his compassions never fail. They are new every morning; great is your faithfulness." (Lamentations 3:21-23 NIV)

Relationship Wisdom Gleaned from my sister Yolanda Livingston

I've had the pleasure of being in relationship with Neesha M. Stringfellow for over forty years. She and I entered the bond of sisterhood/friendship from the age of eight years old until now. We eagerly looked forward to our yearly state-to-state meeting places, chosen by the leaders of our Prayer Band Convention. In the interim, we would write one another letters. We enthusiastically sat waiting at the mailbox in high anticipation of our weekly or bi-weekly letter from the other. We were known, what was referred to many years ago, as pen pals. We continued our contact until later in our teen years. Neesha got married and developed her family, and I lived the single life until age twenty-four. Despite our losing contact for a season, we never lost contact with each other's heart. That's relationship!

I shared the condensed version of our story so I could give clarity to all that I've gleaned from Neesha over the years, as it relates to relationships. I learned that relationship does not mean you have to always be present in each other's face to be present in each other's heart. This is something we learned from the onset together just from her living in Chicago and I in Detroit, but it came alive when we had the break in our connection during our late teens and early twenties. To be present doesn't necessarily mean in person, rather in connection. I also learned that just because you don't see eye to eye on everything, doesn't mean you throw away the bond. The love doesn't go away because we have a disagreement. It doesn't even go away because one may not be available in the way the other would like during certain seasons of life. In essence, don't throw away the baby with the bath water. In many instances, grabbing hold of this mentality makes patience grow, enhances your ability to be forgiving, to love unconditionally, and care selflessly.

Another huge piece of wisdom I gleaned was the importance of listening. Often you must listen for the words behind the words, as well as the words that may never be verbalized. You're learning to be a listener and an observer with this technique. Understanding that it is okay for that to happen from time to time, especially when you know the genuineness of the person. Clarity will always come in the end, and again patience must be exercised. Additionally, in listening, don't hold it against the person. As I stated, this is huge. So many times, people don't take the time to listen. When you listen, you learn, and when you learn, it makes your relationship grow.

Being in a good relationship can teach you a whole lot if you pay attention. It teaches you just how real the Word of God is. The Word says in Proverbs 27:6 (NIV), *"Wounds from a friend can be trusted, but an enemy multiplies kisses."* Sometimes you are not going to hear that you're right in everything that you do. Sometimes you may get that hard, stern correction or truth, but it's only out of love in a true relationship. In like manner, you get to see if the fruit of the spirit is living inside you and in operation. It can live in you but be dormant. True relationship will show you if you are walking in "... *love, joy, peace, longsuffering, gentleness, goodness, faith, meekness, and temperance."* (Galatians 5:22-23 KJV)

It has been a pleasure being in relationship with Neesha over these past years. I have learned so much about relationships, through our trial and error, through her constant presence in my life. The half has not been told here. Thank you, Neesha, for everything. I wouldn't trade this bond for all the tea in China or that million dollars offer.

Take Some Time to Reflect

Final questions to consider after reading this book

What are your expectations in a relationship?

What does a healthy relationship look like to you?

Are you willing to take a look at yourself and see what changes need to be made?

Are you willing to grow?

Is your relationship for a season or a lifetime?

Are you at peace with all of your relationships?

Are people your gift?

Do you shun people?

Do you isolate yourself and try to avoid having relationships? Do you find yourself always having a problem with people?

Does it appear that you are misunderstood, or conversations are somehow misquoted?

Are you easily offended?

Do you feel overwhelmed or taken advantage of?

Why am I loyal to you?

Why is my relationship loyal to you?

Do you have ulterior motives?

Are your 100 percent honest in your relationships?

Are you trustworthy?

What areas do you need healing in relationships?

What do you desire to see change?

Chapter Sixteen

Crazy to Healed

Healing in relationships is always my hope and desire. I sit and pray, listen, read God's word, obey, and then journal. These are good examples to help us remember who God is in our personal lives and helps us keep Him a priority in all of our relationships.

In relationships, everyone has a purpose, and everyone wants to feel validated and affirmed in their purpose, even if there is no awareness.

Everyone needs recognition and affirmation in a relationship. They are looking for it in some kind of way. It may not necessarily be from you, but it has definitely been my observation that people need to be affirmed. As I end this book about relationships, the most important message I would like to give is that everyone in the world is going to be in a relationship with people at some point or another, by choice or by default. Crazy will show up at some point because we are all human. It's so easy to want others to love us, forgive us, and hear our hearts, but when the tables are turned, it's hard to reciprocate the same things we want when we have been hurt in relationships. That's why healing is the key, and a fully surrendered of heart to the creator of relationships matters most. God will heal, we have to choose to say yes to the healing process, sometimes yes to the crazy, while we are waiting on the miracle to happen. God so loved the world. He sent his son to die for us, so that healing can come to all that believe.

His love for us will never leave us or forsake us in our relationships. I believe they are all by God's design. Always remember and reflect those relationships are His idea.

I encourage you as I encourage myself to reflect on all the years that we have been in existence on the earth, let's remember to examine the storms we've been through with people, and also celebrate the victories that we've championed through day by day and moment by moment.

I would also like us to remember that sometimes life can get a little crazy. We are all human and are subject to human nature, which will cause the relationship to seem a little crazy.

This does not mean the crazy that shows up in life does not have purpose. The best gift you have when life presents the uncertain and the disappointment, when you are struggling with the relationships in your life, is to go back to the creator of all life and ask him to show you the purpose in every season. This book has truly been a labor of love through my own personal trials and triumphs.

I thank God for everyone who has helped me to bring it to life.

ജ്ജ

Dear Heavenly Father,

I pray for every person reading this book. I pray that you heal and renew every broken relationship in their lives. I pray for Joy in relationships. I pray that you will drive out the crazy and allow people to be intentional about showing people your love.

Relationships were your idea and thank you.

ജ്ജ

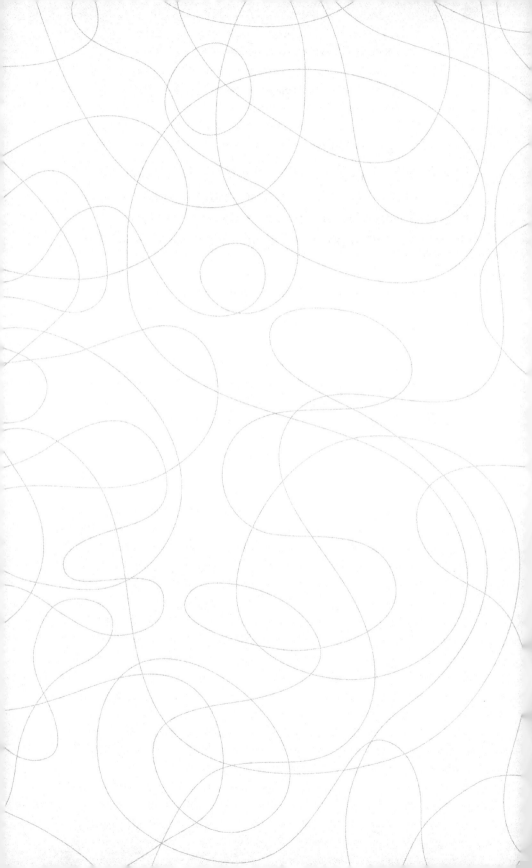

Acknowledgments

My beautiful mom
Dr. Alice Maria Crawford

My daughters
Kristen Maria Dean
Danielle Janae Bonds
Nia Rachel Robinson
Kelani Timaul

My sisters
Cynthia Means
Pastor Shanna Neal
Deborah Anthony
Rachel Jones
Tiffany Crawford

My aunt
Pastor Miriam McFarland

My cousin
Dr. Raquel Robvias

My sister friends
Brenda Baker
Carla Mosley

My childhood sister and friend
Lady Yolanda Livingston

My good friend Tasha Hart
Puzzled to Purpose

My sister friend Marilyn Alexander
Destined to publish

CRUMBLEKNOT

BUILDING MARRIAGES AND FAMILIES THAT DON'T CRUMBLE.

Wes and Neesha are certified life, marriage, family, and relationship coaches. As relationship and marriage coaches, we work with a wide range of people and offer a highly personalized approach tailored to each individual.

In a supportive atmosphere, we help them attain the professional and personal growth they are striving for. We are grateful for the blessing to have seen thousands of marriages enriched and restored.

As Relationship Coaches, we specialize in the following areas:

- Strength Assessments
- Self-Repair
- Personal Growth
- Intimacy
- Professional Development
- Relationship Coaching
- Communication Skills
- Confidence & Personal Power
- Achieving Life Balance
- Health & Weight Issues
- Marketing & Network Consultant

Experience Leadership Certified Coach
John Maxwell Team Certified Coach
Prepare - Enrich Certified Counselor

www.Heartlifetoday.org | www.crumbleknot.com

NEESHA M. STRINGFELLOW

certified life coach

FOCUS • CHANGE • GROW

PREMARITAL / MARITAL COACHING

PROFESSIONAL DEVELOPMENT

RELATIONSHIP COACHING

COMMUNICATION SKILLS

CONFIDENCE / PERSONAL POWER

ACHIEVING LIFE BALANCE

HEALTH / WELLNESS

BUSINESS CONSULTING

WRITING / PUBLISHING

Made in the USA
Monee, IL
23 October 2022

16454853R00096